INDUSTRY
ENGLISH

高等职业教育行业英语系列教材

新编
外贸函电

XINBIAN
WAIMAO HANDIAN

主　编：彭　琳　黄恩成
副主编：谢晓琼　陈鸿莹　邢大成

NEW APPROACH TO
FOREIGN TRADE
CORRESPONDENCES

北京师范大学出版集团
BEIJING NORMAL UNIVERSITY PUBLISHING GROUP
北京师范大学出版社

U0652266

图书在版编目（CIP）数据

新编外贸函电：英文 / 彭琳，黄恩成主编.
北京 ：北京师范大学出版社，2025. 1. -- ISBN 978-7
-303-30587-2

Ⅰ. F75

中国国家版本馆 CIP 数据核字第 2025PP9785 号

出版发行：北京师范大学出版社 https://www.bnupg.com
　　　　　北京市西城区新街口外大街 12-3 号
　　　　　邮政编码：100088
印　　刷：北京天泽润科贸有限公司
经　　销：全国新华书店
开　　本：787 mm×1092 mm　1/16
印　　张：16
字　　数：313 千字
版　　次：2025 年 1 月第 1 版
印　　次：2025 年 1 月第 1 次印刷
定　　价：39.80 元

策划编辑：易　新　　　　　责任编辑：易　新
美术编辑：焦　丽　　　　　装帧设计：焦　丽
责任校对：陈　民　　　　　责任印制：赵　龙

前　言

随着信息技术的飞速发展，国际贸易的方式与手段也在不断革新。作为国际贸易沟通的基本工具，传统外贸函电在时代需求的驱动下，融入了更多数字化与智能化的元素，成为企业拓展国际市场、建立信任、促进贸易合作的关键工具与不可或缺的一环。

基于这一背景，我们精心编写了这本《新编外贸函电》教材。教材以真实外贸企业案例为蓝本，旨在为广大外贸从业者、国际经济与贸易专业学生以及跨境电商专业学生提供一本兼具理论深度与实践指导的学习参考书。

本教材的创新与突破点在于：

1. 真实案例，贴近实战

教材引用了广州蓝尔迪塑料制品有限公司在实际对外业务中的真实案例，涵盖了建立业务关系、询盘与报价、还盘与接受、订单确认、包装、支付方式、装运、索赔与理赔等各个环节。从出口方的角度出发，全方位展示了外贸函电的撰写技巧与实际应用场景，帮助学习者深入理解现代外贸操作流程。

2. 数字赋能，与时俱进

面对数字化转型的浪潮，本教材在保留传统外贸函电写作技巧的同时，融入了微课、电子邮件以及跨境电商即时通讯等内容，充分体现了现代外贸函电课程的数字化特色与应用趋势。

本教材是广东省精品资源共享课程《外贸函电》的配套教材，全书共分为 8 个模块：第 1 模块由黄恩成编写，第 2、第 3、第 6 模块由彭琳编写，第 4、第 8 模块由陈鸿莹编写，第 5、第 7 模块由谢晓琼编写，全书由彭琳统稿。本书的主编和副主编均为广东女子职业技术学院的专业教师。

在教材编写过程中，广州蓝尔迪塑料制品有限公司提供了大力支持，特别是在企业真实案例的分享与指导上，使教材实现了理论与实践的深度融合。学习者在使用本教材时，能够身临其境地感受到对外贸易的真实场景与挑战。在此，我们特别感谢企业专家邢大成老师的鼎力支持与实践指导。

由于编者水平有限，教材中难免存在不足之处，恳请广大读者及同行专家提出宝贵意见，以便我们进一步完善和改进。

主编

2024.7.16

目 录
Contents

Module 1   Fundamentals of Business Correspondence

新编外贸函电

1 Learning Objectives

Upon completion of this module, you should be able to:

- understand business correspondence: its importance, characteristics and considerations;
- grasp the components and formats of business correspondences.

2 Warm-up Questions

- Question 1: What do you know about Business English Writing? Scope? Function? Requirements on the person who writes it?
- Question 2: How many components does a formal business letter usually have?
- Question 3: How to write your name in English?
- Question 4: How to write a date in English? Is/Are there any difference(s) between British style and American style?
- Question 5: How to write an address in English?

新编外贸函电

③ Background Knowledge

微课：外贸函电的重要性

3.1 The Importance of Business Letters

Business correspondence is the backbone of international trade and plays a vital role in establishing and maintaining successful business relationships between organizations and individuals from different countries. Effective communication is essential for every aspect of foreign trade，from negotiating contracts and agreements to resolving disputes and maintaining long-term partnerships，such as **establishing initial contact，negotiating contracts and agreements，building relationships，managing logistics，resolving disputes，maintaining records，marketing and promotion**，etc.

Business correspondence is a critical component of foreign trade and plays a vital role in establishing and maintaining successful business relationships. Effective communication can help to ensure that contracts and agreements are negotiated and managed efficiently，disputes are resolved fairly，and relationships are built and maintained over time. By paying attention to the details of written correspondence and ensuring that messages are conveyed accurately and effectively，organizations can increase their chances of success in the global marketplace.

3.2 Seven C Principles of Business Correspondences

The 7 C's of business correspondence are essential principles designed to enhance the clarity，effectiveness，

微课：7C 原则

and professionalism of written communication in a business context. Here's a detailed explanation of each principle：

(1) Clarity

Definition：Clarity in business correspondence means that the message should be clear and understandable to the recipient. This involves using simple language and avoiding jargon or complex sentences that might confuse the reader.

Example:

Con: "We would like to inform you about the latest developments regarding your account."

Pro: "Here are the recent updates on your account."

(2) Conciseness

Definition: Conciseness means delivering your message in as few words as possible without losing the necessary information. This helps to keep the reader's attention and ensures that your message is straightforward.

Example:

Con: "We would like to take this opportunity to inform you of the fact that your application has been approved."

Pro: "Your application has been approved."

(3) Concreteness

Definition: Concreteness involves providing specific facts and details rather than vague or abstract statements. This makes the message more reliable and easier for the recipient to understand and act upon.

Example:

Con: "We are making improvements to our system."

Pro: "We will upgrade our system on July 15, which will improve processing speed by 30%."

(4) Courtesy

Definition: Courtesy means being respectful and considerate of the recipient's feelings and perspectives. It reflects good manners and helps maintain positive relationships.

Example:

Con: "You missed the deadline."

Pro: "I noticed the deadline was missed. Could you please update us on the status of the project?"

3

(5) Correctness

Definition: Correctness refers to using accurate and grammatically correct language. This ensures that the message is professional and credible.

Con: "You have until the 15th of July complete the task."

Pro: "You have to complete the task before the 15th of July."

(6) Consideration

Definition: Consideration involves putting yourself in the recipient's shoes and tailoring your message to their needs and interests. This principle ensures that the communication is relevant and engaging for the reader.

Example:

Con: "We are pushing for the fulfillment of your order."

Pro: "We understand that you are concerned about the delay in your order. Here's how we're addressing the issue …"

(7) Completeness

Definition: Completeness means providing all necessary information to the recipient so they can fully understand the message and take appropriate action.

Example:

Con: "Please send us the report."

Pro: "Please send us the quarterly sales report by July 15, including the figures for each region and a summary of key trends."

Components of Business Letters

微课：商务信函的组成部分

There are seven essential elements in business letters: letterhead, date, inside address, salutation, body of the letter, complimentary close and, signature. In very formal letters, some other elements may appear, such as reference number, attention line, subject line, identifications, enclosure, copy notation, etc.

The general position of these elements is as following:

Sample 1: Essential elements of business letters with typed letterhead

Sample 1: Essential elements of business letters with typed letterhead

24 Smith Road	1. **Letterhead**
Sunderland	
29th August 2024	
	2. **Date**
Mr. Fred Hattwell	
Manager	
Hattwell Toys Ltd.	
133 Industry Road	3. **Inside address**
Sunderland	
Dear Mr. Hattwell,	
	4. **Salutation**
I am writing to request information about kites, as I have been informed that those produced in your factory are excellent.	
I require all specifications of all models, as well as pricing information. Could you please send the information by first class mail?	5. **Body**
I look forward to your swift reply.	
	6. **Complimentary Close**
Yours sincerely,	
QJ Henberroy	
Ms DESIREE SABRINA HENDERSON	7. **Signature**

新编外贸函电

Sample 2：Letter with all the elements

Electronics Ltd .

3 Stockbridge Road Liverpool   LP5 20M

Tel．：087564789076   Fax：087564747867 ——→ **1.Letterhead**

Website：www. electronics. com. uk

Your Reference：

Our Reference：2569 ——→ **2.Reference number**

Fuji Company ——→ **3.Inside address**

153 Ginza-Chome

Tokyo，Japan

April 13，2024 ——→ **4.Date**

Attention ——→ **5.Attention line**

Dear Sirs， ——→ **6.Salutation**

Re：Portable Colour TV Sets ——→ **7.Subject line**

We have seen your advertisement in the
"Electric Frontier"and are quite interested in
your portable colour television set. ——→ **8.Body**

Enclosed is our Inquiry Note No. 2368. Please
quote us the lowest price C.I.F. Liverpool，stating
the earliest date of shipment.

We look forward to your early reply. ——→ **9.Complimentary close**

Very truly yours， ——→ **10.signature**

Harold Jones

Harold Jones

Manager ——→ **11.Identifications**

HJ/ab ——→ **12.Enclosure**

Encl. : Inquiry Note

CC：Mr. J. L. Smith(New York)← ——→ **13.Copy notation**

4. 1　Letterhead

The letterhead of a business letter contains the return address (usually two or three lines) and appears at the top of the first page. Generally, the letterhead should include the company logo, company's name and full address, telephone number, fax number, E-mail address and, the web address if available.

The letterhead is centered on the page in the indented style, the modified block style and the semi-block styles. It begins at the left margin in the block style.

Sample 3: Letterhead in indented style, modified block and semi-block styles

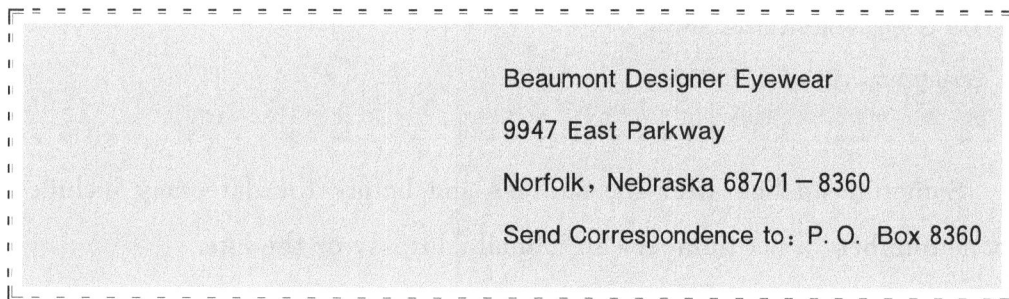

```
                                        Beaumont Designer Eyewear

                                        9947 East Parkway

                                        Norfolk, Nebraska 68701－8360

                                        Send Correspondence to: P. O. Box 8360
```

Sample 4: Letterhead in block style

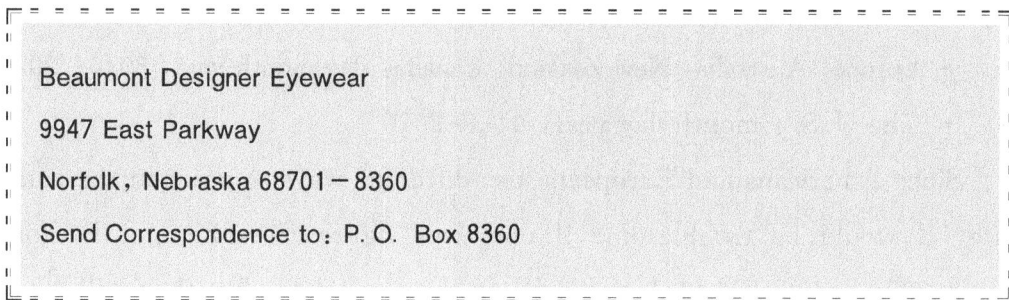

```
Beaumont Designer Eyewear

9947 East Parkway

Norfolk, Nebraska 68701－8360

Send Correspondence to: P. O. Box 8360
```

If the stationery is imprinted with the return address, then the return address may be omitted and the date will occupy the first line in American style.

Sample 5: Letterhead in headed paper in American style

Water Butterfly Co. , Ltd.

No. 14 Avenue des Champs Elysees Paris France
TEL: 8007 E-mail: wff _ summer2008@163. com

September 27, 2024

Panda International Communications Co. , Ltd.

Room 808, 18th Floor

Heping Business Plaza

375 Guangzhou Avenue South

Guangzhou, China 511000

Sometimes a line after the address and before the date may include a phone number, a fax number, an E-mail address, or the like.

4.2   Date

The date tells when the writer writes the letter. There are different ways of writing the date.

- ISO8601 International Standard: year-month-day, 2020-04-30
- Asia Pacific: year-month-day, 2020.04.30
- Europe, Australia, New Zealand, Canada: day-month-year, 30/04/2020
- The U.S. : month-day-year, 04-30-2020

Since Americans and Europeans use different ways to refer to the same date, it would be troublesome if one uses figures for the month, for, 11.08.2024 and 08.11.2024 may refer to the same date, but they will mean completely different dates to Americans and Europeans.

The position of the date depends on the style we use.

1)In British and European correspondences, the date follows the inside address.

Sample 6: Date line in British correspondence

> 3303 West Valley Cove
> Round Rock, Texas 78664
>
> Personnel Assistant
> JD Employee Credit Bank of Texas
> P. O. Box 32345
> Austin, Texas 78745
>
>
> 5 August 2024

In American correspondence, the date follows the sender's address.

Sample 7: Date line in American correspondence

> 3303 West Valley Cove
> Round Rock, Texas 78664
> August 5, 2024
>
> Personnel Assistant
> JD Employee Credit Bank of Texas
> P. O. Box 32345

If the stationery is imprinted with the return address, then the date line will take the first line of the page in American style. (See Sample 5.)

There is a growing tendency to omit the -th, -rd, -nd and -st that follow the date.

4.3   The Inside Address

This is the address the letter is sent to. Make it as complete as possible. Include the title, name, and the routing information. Make sure that the names of the person and the company to whom the letter is written are spelled properly.

Type it flush left and include as many details as necessary, in this order:

- Reader's courtesy title, name, and job title (if the job title is one word)
- Reader's job title (if two or more words)
- Office or department
- Organization name
- Street address/P. O. box/suite/room (comma precedes Northeast or other directional)
- City, state, ZIP code (or city, province, postal code)
- Country (if not in the same country)

When writing to a woman always address her as she signs herself (See Sample 9). It is considered correct to address a woman "Ms." unless she has signed herself "Mrs."

Sample 8: Inside address — to an individual

Dr. Calvin Carson

Cross Country Coach

Dept. of Athletics

Colorado Community College at Cripple Creek

Cripple Creek CO 80678

Sample 9: **Inside address — to an anonymous official in the company**

Sales Manager

Office Systems Pty Ltd.

124 Oak Street

Chatswood NSW 2067

Australia

Sample 10: **Inside address — to a company whose name involves personal names**

Messrs, Kato & Co. , Ltd.

2 Nichome, Ginza Nishi

Chuo-ku, Tokyo

The inside name and address are generally placed four lines below the date line.

4.4   The Salutation

The salutation is the greeting to the reader. It should be typed flush left, three spaces below the last line of the inside address. Here are some ways to write the salutation.

Dear Sirs (British) /Gentlemen (American)—to a company

Dear Sir —to a man if you do not know his name

Dear Madam — to a woman if you do not know her

Dear Mr. Smith — to a man

Dear Mrs. Smith — to a married woman

Dear Miss Smith — to an unmarried woman

Dear Ms. Smith — to a married or unmarried woman

Dear John — to a friend or someone you know well

As the use of the first name in the salutation is an informal practice, it is not recommended for more formal commercial correspondence.

Note that "Gentlemen" is the American way of opening a letter to a company and "Dear Sirs" is the British way. Usually, you can rely on common sense to tell you how to address your reader with respect. When unsure, use the following guidelines and tables to find a fitting title, salutation, and complimentary close that have the same level of formality, as shown in Table 1.

Table 1: **Levels of Formality in Forms of Address**

Level of Formality	Title	Salutations
Formal	Sir/Madame The Honorable	Dear Sir/Madam: Your Excellency:
Standard	Mr. /Ms. /Mrs. / Miss Dr. /Reverend	Dear John/Jane Doe: Dear Mr. /Ms. Doe:
Informal	John/Jane Doe	Dear John/Jane: Jane

4.5   The Body

The body is written as text. A business letter is never hand written. Depending on the letter style chosen, paragraphs may be indented. Regardless of format, skip a line between paragraphs.

The first line of a new paragraph is indented in the indented and the semi block styles. The block and modified block style have all lines of the body to the left margin.

Regardless of style, skip a line between paragraphs.

Skip a line between the greeting and the body.

Skip a line between the body and the close.

4. 6   The Complimentary Close

The complimentary close ends the letter. It begins with a capital letter and ends with a comma, two spaces below the last line of the body. Capitalize only the first word. Begin it slightly to the right of the center of the page, except in full block and block styles.

The way we close a letter depends on how we open it. Table 2 shows the appropriate complimentary close to be used together with various salutations.

Table 2: Proper Forms of Address and Complementary Closings

Level of Formality	Title	Salutations	Complimentary Closings
Formal	Sir/Madame The Honorable	Dear Sir/Madam: Your Excellency:	Very truly yours (American) Yours faithfully (British) Respectfully
Standard	Mr. /Ms. /Mrs. / Miss Dr. /Reverend	Dear John/Jane Doe: Dear Mr. /Ms. Doe:	Yours sincerely Cordially
Informal	John/Jane Doe	Dear John/Jane: Jane	Best wishes Regards

4. 7   Signature

The signature is the signed name or mark of the person who writes the letter or the firm which he or she represents. It is written in ink immediately below the complimentary close.

Skip three spaces and type in the signature line, leaving the space for the printed name of the person to sign the letter.

Note that no courtesy title for a man should be put before the man's name in the signature line except the abbreviations of his academic degrees.

Professional ratings are always typed under the signer's typewritten name or after. In case of the latter, remember to insert a comma between the name and the position.

Women may indicate how they wish to be addressed by placing "Miss", "Mrs. ", "Ms. " or a similar title in parentheses before their name in the signature.

Sample 11: Indications of the writer's address forms

Sincerely yours,

(Signature goes here)

(Mrs.) Elisabeth Jackson

Director of Acquisitions

4.8 Reference Number

A reference number is frequently used in business correspondence. It is used to help in filing by referring to the correspondence that generated our correspondence or to a file number that stands for a new business. Thus, it enables replies to be linked with earlier correspondence and ensures that they reach the right person or department without delay. In American correspondence, the reference number is placed above, below or on the same line as the date, whereas in British correspondence, it is put under the letterhead. Sample 5 above shows the latter case.

4.9 Attention

The attention line is used when the writer, writing to a company, wishes to get it delivered to the proper department or a particular person. It always follows the inside address and precedes the salutation, which for such a letter is "Gentlemen" or "Dear Sirs".

新
编
外
贸
函
电

4.10   Subject

This special part of a letter is used when the writer wants to magnify the importance of the subject, which always follows the salutation and precedes the body of a letter. It may be typed flush with the left margin indented five spaces, or centered on the page. When both an attention line and a subject line are included in a letter, follow the same typing style for each. The introductory word or phrase (Subject or Re) is always followed by a colon.

4.11   Identification Marks

Identification marks are included on almost all business letters, although they are not required. They identify the writer of the letter and the person who typed it. They are mainly for the benefit of the writer and used for administrative purposes. The initials of the signer come first, in all capital letters, followed by the initials of the typist, separated either by a slash (/) or a colon (:).

In American style, identification initials are typed flush with the left margin and follow the signature block.

4.12   Enclosure

The term enclosure is self-descriptive. It means the material other than the letter itself is enclosed. A writer who is enclosing anything in the letter should indicate this by using the word "Enclosure" Enclosure or the abbreviation "Enc." or "Encl." It follows the identification initials. If the enclosure is lost, the recipient will know.

4.13   Carbon Copy Notation

Copies of the letter may be sent to various people, who need to know about the message even though it doesn't pertain to them directly. These may be carbon copies, but most likely they will be photocopied. The notations — Copies to, C (copy), CC (carbon copy), PC (photocopy), or XC (Xerox copy) designate that others are receiving copies. The bc notation, standing for "blind copy", appears on the copy to of the letter, who will read it without the knowledge of the recipient of the original letter.

新编外贸函电

4.14　Postscript

A postscript （P. S. ） is an afterthought，and in a formal letter，it is usually a sign of poor planning. But as a special advice，it has two legitimate functions.

1） Some executives，to add a personal touch to their typewritten letter，occasionally add a postscript in pen and ink.

2） Writers of sales letter often withhold one last convincing argument for emphatic inclusion in a postscript.

Sample 12：Postscript

> P. S. ：See you at the Annual Sales Meeting at the Hillside Plaza on January 10.

⑤ Format of Business Letters

If you look at any collection of letters typically found in business，regardless of their origin and purpose，you might notice they share many of the same characteristics. The addresses and dates appear pretty much in the same place，as do the salutations and complimentary closes. These similarities derive from formats that have been established over time. People have come to expect to see these formats when they look at a business letter. If you give them something they've never seen before，they're likely to think you don't know what you're doing — not a good thing in a competitive business situation. So，in order to communicate effectively you need to conform to your readers' expectations. To that end，this section will illustrate the various business letter formats and discuss their similarities and differences，advantages and disadvantages.

5. 1   Block Style

Water Butterfly Co. , Ltd.

No. 14 Avenue des Champs Elysees Paris France
TEL: 8007 E-mail: wff _ summer2008@163. com

September 27, 2024

Panda International Communications Co. , Ltd.

Room 808, 18th Floor

Heping Business Plaza

375 Guangzhou Avenue South

Guangzhou, China 511450

Dear Sir or Madam,

Your name and address have been given to us by the Hong Kong & Shenzhen Banking Corporation of Nigeria. We are now writing to you for the establishment of business relations.

We have had no contact with your country before. In view of developing friendly relations between our two companies, we wish to ascertain whether cooperation to the advantage of both firms could be established.

We have known that your company is specializing in the export of mobile phones, and we express our desire to trade with you in this line since we are one of the largest mobile phone wholesalers in our country and we are interested in your products. So would you please send us details and prices, possibly also samples, of such goods as we would be interested in?

It is hoped that we start our cooperation on the basis of equality and mutual benefit. We shall be grateful if you will reply at an early date.

Yours faithfully,

Emily Fang

Emily Fang

Purchase Manager

5. 2 Modified Block Style

Panda International Communications Co. , Ltd.
Room 808, 18th Floor Heping Business Plaza
375 Guangzhou Avenue South Guangzhou, China
Tel: 86-020-8005 E-mail: panda _ mobile@tom. com

October 9, 2024

Emily Fang

Purchase Manager

Water Butterfly Co. , Ltd.

No. 14 Avenue des Champs Elysees

Paris France

Dear Emily Fang,

Thank you for your letter of September 27th 2007, inquiring about our range of mobile phones. We feel happy for the opportunity of sending you herewith our catalogue and export price-list.

We also take pleasure in enclosing with this letter a copy of our illustrated brochure, together with our quotation for the Panda mobile phones you requested.

Our terms are payment by an irrevocable L/C at sight against the shipping documents. Delivery can be made 15 days upon our receipt of your order. We allow a 5% discount for orders of 50,000 articles or more and 8% off orders of 100,000 or more.

We should like to point out that all items are available at present and will be sent immediately on receipt of your order and L/C.
We would be glad to offer any further assistance. Please do not hesitate to contact us if you need any additional information.

Yours sincerely,

Reta Xiao

Reta Xiao

Sales Manager

5.3 Semi-Block Style

Water Butterfly Co. , Ltd.

No. 14 Avenue des Champs Elysees Paris France

TEL：8007 E-mail：wff _ summer2008@163. com

October 15，2024

Panda International Communications Co. , Ltd.

Room 808，18th Floor

Heping Business Plaza

375 Guangzhou Avenue South

Guangzhou，China 511450

Dear Miss Xiao，

We are obliged for your offer of October 9th.

We regret that we are unable to accept your offer because the price quoted is high and is not workable. As you may understand，the competition in this market has been as sharp as ever and the present tendency shows that at least three of five most popular brands will be compelled to reduce their retail prices by at least 5％. We regret we can really do nothing unless your prices are adjusted to suit our market.

We therefore hope you will reconsider your offer and find it possible to offer a lower price，calculated on the basis of a monthly order for a minimum of 1,000 sets each type.

We are looking forward to your early reply.

Yours sincerely，

Emily Fang

Emily Fang

Purchase Manager

5.4 Indented Style

Panda International Communications Co., Ltd.
Room 808, 18th Floor Heping Business Plaza
375 Guangzhou Avenue South Guangzhou, China
Tel: 86-020-8005 E-mail: panda _ mobile@tom.com

October 22nd, 2024

Emily Fang, Purchase Manager

Water Butterfly Co., Ltd.

No. 14 Avenue des Champs Elysees

Paris, France

Dear Miss Fang,

Your counter-offer of October 22nd, 2007 has been received. Thank you for your counter-offer.

However, 5% discount for 1,000 items as you requested is too severe for us. We must declare that our quotations are in line with the international market. Because our products are in superb quality, the price will be a little higher than the other suppliers'. One cannot take price separately from quality. If you have taken the quality into account, you will find it reasonable.

We regret that a 5% discount cannot be accepted. But if you can increase your order to 2,000 items, we will consider to giving you a 5% special discount.

We therefore hope you will reconsider our offer and find it possible to accept our price. We are looking forward to your early reply.

Yours sincerely,

Reta Xiao

Reta Xiao

Sales Manager

微课：电子邮件

6 E-mail

E-mail has been adopted by many business professionals. People send out more business E-mails than any other form of business communication. It's faster than the postal service and less expensive than a telephone call. It's more casual than a written letter, but less personal than your own voice. Consequently, E-mail is appropriate when immediacy is desirable and informality is acceptable. Many of the letters discussed in the upcoming chapters may be sent electronically.

However, there is a very significant difference between E-mail and printed mail. E-mail is not private, especially at work. Not only is E-mail stored on the hard drive, at a corporation it is also routinely backed up. E-mail can be forwarded to others, and with the slightest error in the E-mail address, it may be sent to the wrong party. It can, as well, be printed and passed around. For these reasons, not to mention hackers and other security issues, never send a private message through E-mail if you don't want others to see.

Good E-mail writing can lead to business success, while a bad one can harm a professional relationship, sidetrack your project, or cause damage to your reputation. We've become so accustomed to conducting communications by E-mail that we're all bound to be affected from bad E-mail writing both socially and professionally. Following the rules will ensure you benefit from clearer communication and your E-mails get the proper understanding they deserve.

6.1 Parts and Components

E-mail is a substitute of the traditional correspondence, which usually conveys from computer to computer. Sometimes it is also sent and received by mobile phone or PDA (Personal Digital Assistant). Compared with traditional correspondence, we can also send or receive various kinds of attachments in an E-mail, such as photos, formatted documents, music, videos and software programs.

The structures of an E-mail are similar to those of traditional correspondence. It generally contains the following parts:

From/sender — the address of the sender, with the basic form of abc@ xyz. com, usually is inserted by the computer automatically and it's crucial to ensure that all addresses in an E-mail are absolutely correct. If you want to give the receiver a clear appearance, you can set it up with the name of your company.

To/receiver — the address of the recipient.

Date — the date you send your E-mail is also inserted automatically by your computer.

Subject — the main idea of your E-mail message, which is a very important part in the E-mail. A perfect subject will attract the recipient to read your E-mail, especially for the first E-mail to a potential client. When drafting the subject, you can use some abbreviations or tips on this line, such as "RE" (meaning that you are responding to the question); "URGENT" (meaning that this message is time-critical); "FYI" (meaning that it's for your information only and no reply is required); "REQ" (meaning that action is required to taken). And if your message contains an important date, the date should be shown either in the subject or in the body of the E-mail. For instance, Subject: RE: Information for Contract required of Sept. 5.

Body — the message itself and quite similar to the forms of a letter. It contains a salutation, the information you want to convey, and the complimentary close.

Signature — referring to the signature of your E-mail in business. You'd better provide enough information relevant to your business, including your name, title, phone number, fax, Skype number, and the name, address, and website of your company. You can set up your signature in advance to avoid typing it every time.

Enclosure — in foreign transactions, you always send some pictures or documents to your clients, such as the pictures of products, price lists, brochure, shipping documents, etc. So, you can attach them with the E-mail as enclosures.

Carbon Copies (CC) — if you want to send the E-mail to other people besides the recipient, you can use the Carbon Copies, just filling the E-mail address of the person.

6. 2   Basic Guidelines

- First, identify what you want your E-mail to convey. Ask yourself: What outcome do I hope this E-mail brings? What do I want the recipient to do? This will help clarify your intentions.

- Next, decide the recipients of your E-mail. In general, though, avoid sending a message to an entire team of people if you only need to talk to one or two. Similarly, don't CC your boss on all E-mails that don't require their oversight.

- Tailor your subject line. Use a verb or phrase to indicate what action you want the recipient to take, such as " Decision," " Action Required," or "Feedback wanted. "

- When you write your message, start with the action you want the reader to take. Follow up with the context, and end by letting them know you're available for questions. Include visual elements like bullet points, bold text, italics, and shorter paragraphs.

- Always specify the timeline of the action or by when you want the recipient to get back to you. Include the expected end date for the task, request, or feedback.

Here are a few steps that will keep your E-mails clear, concise, and productive.

Step 1: Identify what you want your E-mail to convey.

Before crafting your message, ask yourself: What outcome do I hope this E-mail brings? What do I want the recipient to do?

For instance, are you looking for a status update on a project? Are you trying to secure a time for a one-on-one meeting with a team member? Are you hoping the recipients will participate in your survey?

Pro tip: As you begin writing, think of your words as the call to action that you want your recipients to perform. This mindset will help you craft a message with clear intention.

Step 2: Edit your recipient list.

Before you put a pen to paper (or fingers to keyboard), carefully select who you need to perform the outcome you've identified. If you're looking to schedule a one-on-one meeting, for instance, the required recipient will be obvious. But if you're looking for a status update on a project, you may need to be more thoughtful when putting together your recipient list.

Ask yourself: Who has the information I'm looking to acquire? Will one team member be able to share it with me, like a team leader or a project manager? Or do I need to include multiple team members? If so, who is absolutely necessary to include? Who isn't?

If you want to include someone just as an FYI or, CC a person to keep them in the loop, write a short note in the E-mail thread when you add new recipients, so everyone has context. In general, though, avoid sending a message to an entire team of people if you only need to talk to one or two. Similarly, don't CC your boss on all E-mails that don't require their oversight.

Knowing who the E-mail is for will help you craft a more personalized message.

Pro tip： When responding to E-mails，set your default to "Reply" rather than "Reply all" so you don't flood people's inboxes unnecessarily.

Step 3：Tailor your subject line.

In the age of infinite scrolling，most of us are quickly scanning the text in our inboxes and prioritizing messages that feel critical to respond to. You need a standout subject line to get your E-mail noticed. A clear subject line can also serve as a "north star" and help you stay on track when crafting the body of the message.

Here are a few examples of strong vs. weak subject lines that you can emulate and adjust for your own message.

Example 1： You want your boss to make a decision on your proposal.

Weak：New Marketing Strategy

Strong：Decision Required：New Marketing Strategy

Example 2： You need action from a team member to meet a project deadline.

Weak：Update on Project

Strong：Action Required：Project Information required by 1 pm on Tues （Aug 16）

Example 3： You want a colleague to provide feedback.

Weak：Concept Note

Strong：Feedback：Concept Note

Step 4：Craft your message.

To keep your reader's attention，your message must be as clear as your subject line. To do that，keep the message short and to the point. While the exact length of your E-mail will depend on your call-to-action，and how much context you need to explain it，your goal is to structure the information in a way that's easy for the reader to understand.

Start with the action you want them to take，follow up with the context of why you require that action，and then end by letting them know you're

新编外贸函电

available for questions. Visual elements like bullet points，bold text，italics，and shorter paragraphs（two to three sentences long）may make your message easier to read quickly and digest.

Example 1：Weak

Dear Pam，

I wanted to bring to your attention a number of issues that we've been having with our content management system. They're creating a range of issues for people on my team.

Many of us are having trouble logging into the system. After entering our credentials into the log in window，it's taking a long time to access，and the screen has been consistently freezing on us or going blank. I've had one staff member tell me that it's taken him 15 minutes to log in and another mention that it took them almost 20 minutes to log in.

In addition，when staff log in，we're unable to access the "create draft" option. When we click on that，it takes us to "archive" posts and we don't know how to resolve this. All of this is causing a lot of frustration among the team members. So，I recommend we meet and identify why these issues are occurring and how to fix them.

Thanks，

Jo

Example 2：Strong

Dear Pam，

I'm reaching out to set up a call today at 2 pm to discuss some of the ongoing software issues with our content management system that are causing a lot of delays for my team.

We've identified two major issues.

1. Log-in issues: Many of my team members have reported that their computer screens are freezing or turning blank when they log onto the website. For others, it's taking 15—20 minutes to log in.

2. Unable to create draft: When we click "create draft," we are being redirected to the archives folder.

I'm blocking some time on our calendars to talk in detail about these concerns. Hope that is okay.

Please do let me know if you'd like me to collect any additional information before our meeting.

Thanks.

Jo

Step 5: Specify Timelines.

All too often, we send out E-mails asking people to complete a request without giving them a timeline. This is a mistake. When we fail to tell people when we need something, we put it on them to decide whether the task is urgent or not. To avoid this confusion, specify when you want the recipient to get back to you at the beginning of your E-mail. Include the expected end date for the task, request, or feedback.

For example:

- Could you please fill out this survey by Friday, July 15 at 3 pm?
- Please share any feedback you have on my report by EOD tomorrow.
  If you need more time, just let me know and I can adjust.
- Can you please gather the data we discussed for a 10 am meeting on Monday, August 10?

Pro tip: If your E-mail application allows it, set a two-minute delay on all outgoing E-mails. This gives you a couple of minutes of buffer time to retract or edit an E-mail if you want to, and can be a lifesaver when you inevitably, accidentally hit "send" on an E-mail draft, or send it to the wrong recipient.

Learning these E-mail practices will make you come across as more thoughtful, clear, and concise while communicating with your boss, peers, and colleagues.

6.3 Points to Check before Sending an E-mail

E-mail may be your initial point of contact with someone and because of that, it's your first opportunity to make an impression. Take great care in composing your messages. Before you hit the "send" button, answer these 7 questions.

(1) Is my message error free?

Checking your E-mail for mistakes is the most important thing you can do before you send it. Incorrect spelling and bad grammar will make you look careless. That goes against the impression you are trying to make, especially if you are applying for a job.

Proofread until you are confident you have caught all spelling and grammatical errors, as well as typos.

(2) What does my E-mail address say about me?

Your work E-mail address — which, by the way, you should never use for job searching — is probably very straightforward. Most likely it is some variant of your name. You may have chosen a less business-like address to use for personal E-mail. An address that is suggestive, childish, or cute is okay if you are only using it to send messages to your friends and family, but if you need to write a professional E-mail, sign up for a new account that conveys professionalism.

Set up an E-mail address that uses your actual name. Try your first and last names; your first name, middle initial, and last name; or some combination of those. Never send your professional E-mail from chickybabe @mymail. com.

(3) Are the name and E-mail address in the "To" field correct?

When you begin typing a recipient's name into the "To" field, most E-mail clients will fill in the rest of the name with one from your contacts. You could easily end up with the wrong name in that field so make sure to pay attention to this.

Imagine what trouble might arise if you accidentally send an E-mail to the wrong recipient. Let's say you are looking for a job while you are still employed. A hiring manager at a prospective employer could have a name that begins with the same letter as your current boss's name. How embarrassing would it be if you sent your boss a message meant for that hiring manager? Not only do you want to make sure your message reaches its intended destination, but you also want to be certain it doesn't reach an unintended one.

(4) Have I used the proper title to address the recipient?

If you are already on a first-name basis with the person you are E-mailing, it is okay to address them that way in your message. However, if this is your first time communicating with someone, or you aren't sure how they prefer to be addressed, it is preferable to use a formal title like Mr. , Ms. , Mrs. , or Dr. and the recipient's last name.

Always err on the side of caution. It can't hurt to be formal. For a hint about how someone with whom you already have an established relationship prefers to be addressed, look back on prior messages to see how they are signed. That will help you decide what to do.

(5) Does my tone convey my message well?

As the saying goes, "It's not what you say but how you say it. " When you speak to someone face-to-face, you can rely on intonation, body language, and facial expression to help give additional meaning to your words.

When you try to convey the same message in writing, there is more room for misunderstanding because the reader can't see your face, read your body language, or hear your voice. Make sure your message is polite and sounds friendly, and that your intended meaning is clear.

(6) Is my message simple, but not cryptic?

Keeping your messages short and sweet will make them easier to understand. At the same time, you should not omit anything important. You don't want to force the recipient of your E-mail to guess what you are trying to say. Your message should be as precise as possible but include all the necessary information.

(7) Have I included unsolicited attachments?

Many people refuse to open E-mail attachments they aren't expecting. They are right to avoid doing that. Computer viruses are often transmitted in those attachments. If you want to send a file to someone, for example, your resume, ask your recipient for his permission first. Send it only if he says it is okay.

⑦ Company Profile

微课：公司简介撰写

7.1 Significance of Company Profiles

Company profiles serve as a concise yet comprehensive introduction to businesses, encapsulating their history, culture, vision, and strategic objectives. They are essential in aiding stakeholders, including potential

新
编
外
贸
函
电

clients, investors, and partners, to quickly grasp the essence and direction of a company. By articulating the company's core values, mission, and unique selling propositions, profiles foster a sense of trust and credibility. Furthermore, company profiles can differentiate a business from its competitors, highlighting its strengths and market position. They often include information on leadership, organizational structure, financial health, and achievements, offering a snapshot of the company's overall performance and potential for growth. In an increasingly competitive landscape, a well-crafted company profile can be a powerful tool for branding and marketing, helping to attract and retain customers, as well as secure new business opportunities.

Writing a company profile is an essential task for any business, as it serves as a professional introduction to potential clients, partners, investors, and employees. A well-crafted company profile not only informs but also engages the reader, highlighting the company's values, achievements, and vision. Here's a step-by-step guide to help you write an effective company profile:

7.2　Guidelines for Compiling a Company Profile

(1)Define Your Purpose and Audience

- Why are you creating this profile? (e. g. , attract investors, generate leads, recruit talent)
- Who is your target audience? (e. g. , potential clients, venture capitalists, job seekers)
- What key message do you want to convey? (e. g. , innovation, customer focus, market leadership)

(2)Structure Your Content

While the length and specific sections may vary, a typical company profile includes the following parts.

- Cover Page: Company name, logo, tagline (optional), contact information

- Table of Contents: (For longer profiles)
- Executive Summary: A concise and compelling overview of your company, highlighting its mission, values, unique selling points, and achievements. Keep it brief (1-2 paragraphs).
  - ➢ Company Overview:
- Company Overview Mission and Vision: Clearly state your company's purpose and long-term aspirations.
- Values: Outline the core principles guiding your business practices.
- History: Briefly narrate the company's journey, highlighting key milestones and achievements.
  - ➢ Products/Services:
- Describe your offerings in detail, focusing on their benefits and value propositions.
- Use high-quality images and visuals to showcase your products/ services.
  - ➢ Target Market:
- Define your ideal customer or client base.
- Explain how your products/services address their specific needs and pain points.
  - ➢ Competitive Advantages:
- Clearly articulate what sets you apart from competitors.
- Highlight your unique strengths, innovations, or competitive pricing.
  - ➢ Team/Leadership:
- Showcase your team's expertise and experience.
- Include brief biographies of key personnel, highlighting their skills and accomplishments.
  - ➢ Financial Highlights: (Optional, mainly for investors)
- Provide key financial data like revenue, growth rate, and profitability.

- Include charts and graphs for visual representation.

- Testimonials & Case Studies:

- Build credibility and trust by featuring positive client testimonials.

- Showcase successful projects or case studies demonstrating your capabilities.

  ➤ Call to Action:

- Clearly state what you want the reader to do next.

- Provide contact information and links to relevant web pages.

(3)Writing Style and Tone

- Keep it concise and engaging: Use clear and concise language, avoiding jargon and technical terms.

- Focus on benefits, not just features: Explain how your products/ services solve customer problems and deliver value.

- Use a professional tone: Maintain a formal and professional writing style throughout the profile.

- Proofread carefully: Ensure the document is free of grammatical errors and typos.

(4)Visual Appeal

- Use high-quality visuals: Incorporate professional images, graphics, and charts to enhance engagement.

- Maintain consistent branding: Ensure your company logo, colors, and fonts are consistent throughout the profile.

- Choose a professional layout: Use a clean and modern design template for a polished look.

7.3   Sample Company Profiles

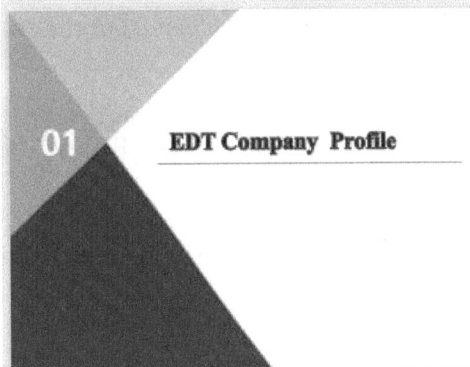

Fig 1: EDT Company Profile (in PPT form)

Safety Pool Cover   Automatic Pool Cover   Bubble Pool Cover   Manual Roller   Pool Liner   Solid PVC Pool Cover

Landy (Guangzhou) Plastic Products Co., Ltd. was founded in 2000 by M. Xinke Du, with its headquarter located in Nansha, Guangzhou, a national-level free trade zone. It is an industry corporation with business in product research and development, production, sales and service. It owns two factories, one 16,000-square-meter factory in Guangzhou and another 42,000-square-meter branch in Yangjiang.

Landy has got the quality management system certification of ISO9001 (2015) and environmental management system certification of ISO14001. It was rated as high-tech enterprises. With independent R & D team, Landy has mastered the industrys core technology and has obtained 16 patents. With the standard of "quality is the core, customer satisfaction is the purpose", Landy tries its best to provide high-quality products and services to our valued customers. Landy owns "LANDY", "POOL-LINER", and "TC-COVER" three independents brands, and its products have passed CE, AWTA, ASTM, SGS, CQC, CNAS, IQNET and other professional certifications.

Fig 2: Landy (Guangzhou) Plastic Products Co., Ltd. Profile

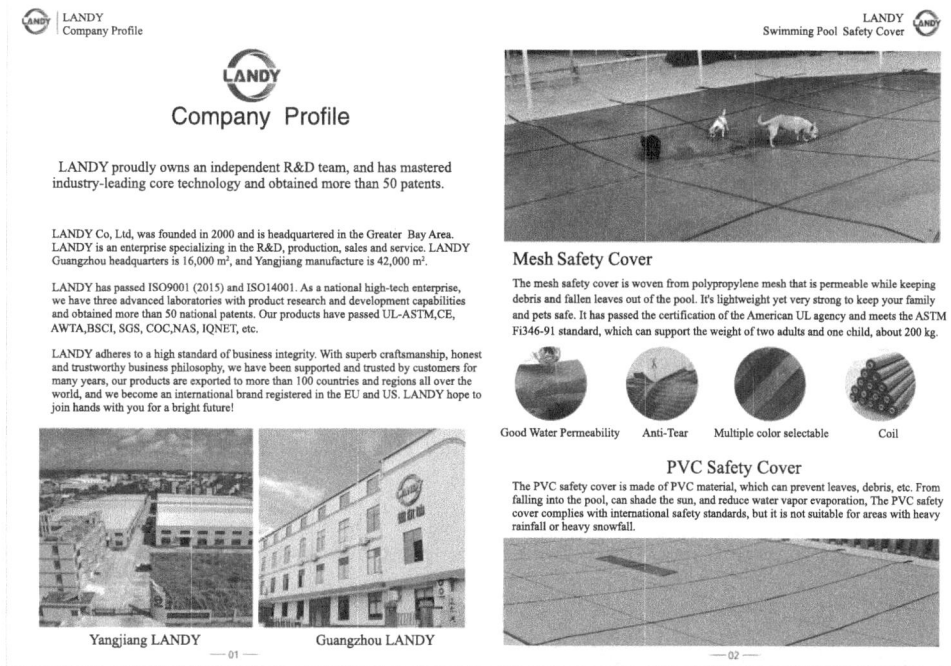

Fig 3：Page 2 of Landy (Guangzhou) Plastic Products Co. , Ltd. Profile

Landy (Guangzhou) Plastic Products Co. , Ltd. was founded in 2000, headquartered in the National Nansha Free Trade Zone in southern Guangzhou. It is an industry corporation engaged in product research and development, production, sales and service. Currently, it owns two factories, one 16,000-square-meter factory in Nansha and another 42,000-square-meter branch in Yangjiang, Guangdong.

Landy has obtained the quality management system certification of ISO9001 (2015) and the environmental management system certification of ISO14001. It was rated as a high-tech enterprise, having mastered the industry's core technology and obtained 16 patents. With the principle of "quality is the core, customer satisfaction is the purpose", Landy tries its best to provide high-quality products and services to our valued customers. Landy owns three independents brands, namely, "LANDY", "POOL-LINER" and "TC-COVER". Its products have passed CE, AWTA, ASTM, SGS, CQC, CNAS, IQNET and other professional certifications.

⑧ Field Exploring

- Foreign trade elite literacy: E-mail Etiquettes
- Be mindful of E-mail security and avoid opening suspicious attachments or clicking on unknown links.
- Respect others' time by responding to E-mails promptly, even if it's just to acknowledge receipt.
- If you cannot answer immediately, write a brief note and explain why. It will create goodwill.
- Use a clear and concise subject line that accurately reflects the content of your E-mail.
- Begin with a proper salutation, such as "Dear [Name]," or "Hello [Name]," depending on the level of formality.
- Use a professional and friendly tone throughout the E-mail.
- Keep your message brief and to the point, focusing on the main purpose of your communication.
- Use proper grammar, spelling, and punctuation to ensure clarity and professionalism.
- Break your E-mail into paragraphs for better readability, especially if the content is lengthy.
- Avoid using all caps, as it can be perceived as shouting.
- Be cautious with humor or sarcasm, as they may be misinterpreted without facial expressions or tone of voice.
- Double-check attachments, if any, to ensure they are included and properly named.
- Use "Reply All" only when necessary to avoid cluttering others' inboxes.
- Proofread your E-mail before sending it to catch any errors or unclear statements.

- Include a proper closing，such as "Best regards," "Sincerely," or "Thank you," followed by your name.
- Use a professional E-mail signature that includes your contact information.

9 Practice：Please Rearrange the Following in Order.

No.	Contents
a	750008
b	Dear Miss Fang
c	December 10th，2007
d	Emily Fang
e	No. 14 Avenue des Champs Elysees
f	Paris，France
g	Purchase Manager
h	Reta Xiao
i	Sales Manager
j	Thank you for your L/C dated December 3rd，2007. We are now writing to confirm our fax dispatched just now informing you that your P/C No. 201ZCBE3012 dated Dec，3rd for 2000pcs No. P1001 Mobile called "Panda P95" has been shipped today from Guangzhou by vessel May Flower，which is due to arrive at your port on or about January 20th. We have drawn a draft at sight for the invoice amount under the French Bank，Paris L/C No. 2525 through China Bank，Guangzhou to whom all documents have been handed. Enclosed please find copies of following documents：2 Non-negotiable B/L；1 Commercial Invoice No. 0932；1 Insurance Policy；1 Inspection Certificate； We shall be pleased to hear in due course that the consignment has arrived safely and in good order.
k	Water Butterfly Co. , Ltd
l	Yours Sincerely，

新编外贸函电

Module 2 Developing Customers

微课：开发客户

① Learning Objectives

Upon completion of this module，you should be able to：

- learn how to develop a business and acquire customers；

- be able to write RFQs and replies；

- learn how to structure a letter for establishing business relations；

- be familiar with relevant business documents.

② Warm-up Questions

- Question 1：What are the channels for developing customers? How to promote a company's products?

- Question 2：What information should the inquiry letter include?

- Question 3：How to reply to an enquiry E-mail?

③ Background Knowledge

微课：询盘与回复

新编外贸函电

Establishing business relations is the first step in enlarging a company's business and developing mutual trade with new customers. It is fundamental in foreign trade and in international exchange because transaction can only be made after the business connections have been set up. For a newly established firm or an old one that wishes to expand its market and enlarge its business scope and turnover, to seek prospective clients and establish business relations is one of the most important measures.

Before establishing business relations, we must be well familiar with customers' situations such as credit standing, trading scope, operating ability, and their attitude towards us. In international trade, we may obtain business information about firms and companies in other countries through following channels：

(1) Banks

(2) Chamber of Commerce

(3) Business associates of the same trade

(4) Commercial Counselor's Office

(5) Commercial Office of a Foreign Embassy

(6) Media advertising

(7) Exhibitions and trade fairs

(8) Market survey

(9) Recommendation by a business friend or a client

(10) Web research

➤ What Is an Inquiry Letter?

An inquiry is a request for information about a product. In foreign trade, an importer wishes to buy a commodity will ask an exporter the sale of the commodity and the terms of trade.

In an inquiry letter, there is a benefit to both the seller and the buyer. In it, the buyer asks for some information and some help. The buyer also provides an incentive encouraging the seller to act. An inquiry letter may include the following information related to the product: quality, quantity, name, specification, time of shipping, packing, terms of payment, and so on. In order to obtain the necessary information, the inquirers should state clearly and concisely what information he needs.

➤ Inquiry Generally Falls into Two Types

1) General Inquiry: This inquiry is not necessarily related to the specific transaction, is generally less detailed. In a general inquiry, the writer asks only for catalogs, price lists or samples in order to get some general knowledge of the products.

2) Specific Inquiry: A specific inquiry is actually a request for what is sometimes called an offer (or a request for an offer). In other words, the buyer intends to buy a commodity, or already has a ready buyer, asking the seller to bid on this commodity. In a specific inquiry, the buyer wants the seller to provide more detailed information of a particular product.

4 Module-Related Correspondence

Letters Concerning Inquiry and Reply
➤ Request for Establishing Business Relations
➤ General Enquiry Letter
➤ Specific Enquiry Letter

5 Sample Letters

微课：建立贸易关系

Case 1

广州蓝尔迪塑料制品有限公司外贸业务员 Leo 了解到英国客户 Cathy 所在的公司需要订购 Solar Swimming Pool Cover（太阳能泳池盖）这类产品，Leo 给 Cathy 发出了建立贸易关系的信函。

Request for Establishing Business Relations

March 3，2019

Dear Sirs，

We learn from our Commercial Office in your country that you are a large buyer of "POOL-LINER" and "TC-COVER" on pool security protection field. As articles of this kind fall within the scope of our business activities，we take this opportunity to express our wish to enter into business relations with you.

Our company's products are known for their good quality，attractive designs and fine workmanship. Our company（Landy）has occupied most of the domestic and foreign market share. We believe that through our joint efforts they will also meet with a favorable reception in your country.

In our trade with merchants of various countries，we always adhere to the principle of equality and mutual benefit. The policy of ours greatly helps to strengthen trade relations and promote friendship between the Chinese people and the people of other countries. We are sure of good business prospects before us.

In order to give you a general idea of our "POOL-LINER" and "TC-COVER"，we are sending you，under separate cover，a copy of the latest catalogue. If you find any of the items interesting，please let us know as soon as possible. We shall be glad to send you quotations and samples upon receipt of your detailed enquiry. Your rapid specific enquiry will be appreciated.

Yours faithfully，

Leo

Leo

Common Expressions

- Commercial office 商业办公室
- POOL-LINER 泳池衬垫
- TC-COVER 泳池盖
- pool security protection 泳池安全保护
- business activities 商业活动
- business relations 商业关系
- good quality 高质量
- attractive designs 吸引人的设计
- fine workmanship 精湛的工艺
- market share 市场份额
- favorable reception 受欢迎
- equality and mutual benefit 平等互利
- trade relations 贸易关系
- promote friendship 促进友谊
- good business prospects 良好的商业前景
- catalogue 目录
- quotation 报价
- sample 样品
- detailed enquiry 详细询价
- rapid specific enquiry 快速具体的询价

Useful Expressions

- take this opportunity to express our wish to … 借此机会表达我们希望……
- known for … 以……而闻名
- occupy … market share 占据……市场份额
- through our joint efforts 通过我们的共同努力
- meet with a favorable reception 受到欢迎
- adhere to the principle of … 坚持……的原则

- greatly help to … 大大有助于……

- be sure of … 确信……

- give you a general idea of … 给你一个关于……的大致了解

- under separate cover 另函附上

- let us know as soon as possible 尽快让我们知道

- upon receipt of … 在收到……之后

- be appreciated 感激/赞赏

Writing Tips：

Structure of Letter for Establishing Business Relations

After getting the desired names，addresses and other related information of the business partners，one may start sending a letter to establish business relations. In such cases，the writer usually informs his addressee of the following：

➢ **Beginning：**Source of information；

State how you obtained relevant information of the other party.

➢ **Body：**Company introduction and intention；

1）Company introduction：Offer a brief introduction to the company and it's products.

2）Intention：state your willingness to establish business relations with the other party and remind of the attached documents such as samples，price lists，catalogs，etc.

3）Guarantee of credit and reference：give the reference as to the company's financial position and integrity. Tell the other party where to inquire your credit，especially the main transaction banks.

➢ **Ending：**Express the appreciation of an early reply.

Case 2

广州蓝尔迪塑料制品有限公司外贸业务员 Leo 收到了一封英国客户 Cathy 的一般询盘信函，询问 POOL-LINER and TC-COVER（泳池衬垫和泳池盖）这类产品的信息。

General Enquiry for POOL-LINER and TC-COVER

May 8，2019

Dear Leo，

We have got your letter dated March 3，2019 and learned that you manufacture and export a variety of"POOL-LINER"and"TC-COVER".

Our company is one of the importers of such articles in London. As there is a steady demand for high quality "POOL-LINER" and"TC-COVER"，we would like you to send us as soon as possible your illustrated catalogue，price-list and all necessary information about the goods.

We are large dealers in "POOL-LINER" and"TC-COVER"and believe there is a promising market in our area for moderately priced goods of the above mentioned. Your prompt attention will be much appreciated.

Yours faithfully，

Cathy

Cathy

Common Expressions

- importer 进口商
- illustrated catalogue 图文并茂的目录
- price-list 价格表
- dealer 经销商
- moderately priced 价格适中的
- promising market 有前景的市场

Useful Expressions

- manufacture and export 制造并出口
- a variety of 各种各样的
- steady demand 稳定的需求
- send … as soon as possible 尽快发送……

- all necessary information about the goods 关于货物的所有必要信息

- appreciate 感激，重视

- prompt attention 迅速关注/回复

- believe there is … 相信有······

- Your prompt attention will be much appreciated. 您的及时关注将不胜感激。

Case 3

广州蓝尔迪塑料制品有限公司外贸业务员 Leo 收到了一封英国客户 Cathy 的具体询盘信函，询问 Solar Swimming Pool Cover(太阳能游泳池盖) 系列产品的信息。

Specific Enquiry for Solar Swimming Pool Cover

May 10，2019

Dear Leo，

Nice to meet you during last Guangzhou Fair.

We are now interested in Solar swimming pool cover in bulk quantities，and shall be pleased if you send us ASAP your illustrated catalogs，latest price-list with quantities available and samples. And in your reply，please indicate the earliest date of shipment as well as your best quantity discount.

Your rapid reply will be appreciated.

Yours faithfully，

Cathy

Cathy

Common Expressions

- Guangzhou Fair 广交会

- bulk quantities 大批量

- illustrated catalogs 图文并茂的目录

- latest price-list 最新价格表

- quantities available 可供应数量

新编外贸函电

- earliest date of shipment 最早发货日期
- quantity discount 批量折扣

🔵 Useful Expressions

- Nice to meet you … 很高兴在……见到你
- We are now interested in … 我们现在对……感兴趣
- send us ASAP … 请尽快发送给我们……
- in your reply，please indicate … 请在您的回复中注明……
- be pleased if … 如果……将不胜感激
- with quantities available 与可供应数量一起

🔵 Writing Tips

Structure of Enquiry Letters：

➢ State the source of the information and make a self-introduction at the beginning of the letter.

➢ State the purpose of writing the letter. For example，the writer may explain to the recipient what he wants，give a description or specification of the goods he requires or express his willingness to enter into business relations with the recipient，etc.

➢ End the letter by expressing the expectation for an early reply.

Case 4

广州蓝尔迪塑料制品有限公司外贸业务员 Leo 回复了英国客户 Cathy 的具体询问 Solar Swimming Pool Cover 系列产品的询盘信函。

微课：卖家发盘函

Letter 1：Reply to the Specific Enquiry for Solar Swimming Pool Cover

May 28，2019

Dear Cathy，

Thank you for your enquiry of May 10，2019. Meanwhile，we enclose details of our Solar Swimming Pool Cover for your examination.

All the models illustrated can be supplied from stock at competitive prices, shown on the price-list inside the catalogue. As we carry a large stock of the goods in superior quality, we can execute your commands promptly and faithfully, at the rock-bottom prices as shown in the price-list.

We guarantee shipment within 10 days of receipt of your order.
We are looking forward to your early order.

Yours sincerely,

Leo

Leo

Common Expressions

- examination 检查

- model 型号

- stock 库存

- competitive prices 有竞争力的价格

- price-list 价格表

- superior quality 优质

- execute 执行

- commands 订单

- rock-bottom prices 最低价

- shipment 发货

Useful Expressions

- Thank you for your enquiry of … 感谢您于……的询问

- Meanwhile, we enclose … 同时, 我们附上……

- All the models illustrated can be supplied from stock 所有图示型号均可从库存中供应

- at competitive prices 以有竞争力的价格
- We guarantee shipment within ... days of receipt of your order 我们保证在收到您订单后的……天内发货
- We are looking forward to your early order 我们期待您早日下单
- promptly and faithfully 迅速且可靠地
- at the rock-bottom prices 以最低价

Letter 2：Reply to the Specific Enquiry for Solar Swimming Pool Cover

Landy（Guangzhou）Plastic Products Co.，Ltd.

Add：No. 215 Shipai Industrial Zone，Dongchong Town，

Nansha District，Guangzhou，China，Guangzhou，

Guangdong，China

Company website：https://www.poolcoveraaa.com/

October 9th，2019

Cathy，Purchase Manager

Water Butterfly Co.，Ltd

223 George St，Sydney NSW 2000

Dear Cathy，

Thank you for your letter of September 27th 2019，inquiring about our range of Solar Swimming Pool Cover. We feel happy for the opportunity of sending you here with our catalogue and export price-list.

We also take pleasure in enclosing with this letter a copy of our illustrated brochure，together with our quotation for the Solar Swimming Pool Cover you requested.

Our terms are payment by an irrevocable L/C at sight against the shipping documents. Delivery can be made 15 days upon our receipt of your order. We allow a 5% discount for orders of 50 articles or more and 8% off orders of 100,000 or more.

We should like to point out that all items are available at present and will be sent immediately on receipt of your order and L/C.

We would be glad to offer any further assistance. Please do not hesitate to contact us if you need any additional information.

Yours sincerely

Leo

Leo

Sales Manager

Common Expressions

- export price-list 出口价格表

- illustrated brochure 图文并茂的小册子

- quotation 报价单

- irrevocable L/C at sight 不可撤销即期信用证

- shipping documents 装运单据

- discount 折扣

- available 可获得的

- further assistance 进一步的帮助

- additional information 额外信息

- payment terms 付款条件

- delivery 交货

Useful Expressions

- Thank you for your letter of [date]. 感谢您的来信，日期为[具体日期]。

- inquiring about ... 询问关于……

- We feel happy for the opportunity of ... 我们很高兴有机会……

- enclose with this letter … 随信附上……

- Our terms are … 我们的条款是……

- Delivery can be made … 交货可以在……进行

- We allow a [percentage]% discount for orders of [quantity] or more. 对于订单数量达到或超过[具体数量]，我们提供[百分比]%的折扣。

- All items are available at present … 所有商品目前都有货……

- We would be glad to offer any further assistance. 我们很乐意提供任何进一步的帮助。

- Please do not hesitate to contact us if you need any additional information. 如果您需要任何额外信息，请随时与我们联系。

Writing Tips

How to Respond to an Inquiry Letter：

➤ You should indicate the inquiry that was made, as you understand it.

➤ Express your appreciation for the person's interest.

➤ If possible，personally respond to the inquiry. You might want to include with your response letter any brochures，catalogs，reports，or other helpful information available.

➤ If you cannot personally answer the person's question, let him/her know that you have contacted the person who can and that he/she will shortly be in touch with the reader. If this is not possible，express your regret for being unable to help the reader，and try to find out for him/her the contact information for someone who can help.

➤ If appropriate，you might want to include additional information about your organization，the products or services you sell，or the subject matter of the inquiry，beyond the scope of the original inquiry.

➤ Close by saying that you would be happy to help the other party in the future if he/she needs further assistance or by wishing him/her well in his/her endeavor or project，etc.

6 Field Exploring

➤ **Supplemental Expressions**

1. We have your name and address from the Commercial Counselor's Office of your Embassy in Beijing and are now writing to you for the establishment of business relations.

我们从贵国驻京使馆商务参赞处得悉贵公司行名和地址，现特致函与贵公司建立业务关系。

Similar structures：

We have obtained …

We come to know …

We heard …

We owe your
| name and address |
| fax number |
| business scope |
| products |
| E-mail address |
to …

2. We have learned by courtesy of Mr. Greenhorn that you are one of the leading importers of Chinese chemicals and pharmaceutics in your country.

承蒙格林豪先生介绍，我们得知你们是贵国中国化工产品和药品的主要进口商之一。

Similar structures :

We understood
from the BOC Beijing
through the courtesy of CCIEC
on the recommendation of …
after contacting your trade delegation
that …

3. Your firm has been recommended to us by Bank of China in Beijing.

在北京的中国银行已把贵公司介绍给我们。

Similar structures :

Your name has been
recommended
introduced
suggested
brought forward given
to us by …

4. We have the pleasure of introducing ourselves to you as a state-operated corporation dealing exclusively in light industrial goods.

我们有幸自荐，我们是一家专营轻工产品的国有公司。

Similar structures :

We
have the pleasure to introduce
take the pleasure in introducing
take the liberty of introducing
avail ourselves of this opportunity to introduce
are venturing to write to introduce
wish to introduce
ourselves to you …

It
is of
gives us
great pleasure to introduce ourselves to you …

5. We are the chief cigarette packing materials exporter in Austria and are thankful to the Chinese Embassy in Vienna for giving your name.

我们是奥地利主要的香烟原辅材料出口商，并感谢驻维也纳的中国使馆向我们提供了你们的行名。

Similar structures：

We are
| thankful |
| grateful |
| obliged |
| indebted |
to … for giving us your name and address.

6. Specializing in the export of Chinese arts & crafts goods，we express our desire to trade with you in this line.

我们专营中国工艺美术品出口，愿与贵方进行交易。

Similar structures：

| Specializing |
| Being experienced |
| Having been for years |
| Dealing exclusively |
in the export of …

7. We are willing to enter into business relations with your company on the basis of equality and mutual benefit.

我们愿在平等互利的基础上与贵公司建立业务关系。

Similar structures：

We are
| willing |
| desirous |
| glad |
| more than pleased |
| keen |
| ready |
| eager |
| anxious |
to establish business relations with you.

We are pleased to

| establish a direct trade connection / relations |
| enter into business activities |
| have an opportunity of cooperating |
| explore the possibility of developing trade |

with you.

8. Being closely connected with reliable suppliers here, we shall be able to do considerable export business with you.

我公司与本地可靠的供应商联系密切，能与贵公司做可观的出口生意。

Similar structures:

Being closely connected with reliable

| suppliers |
| wholesalers |
| customers |
| manufacturers |
| distributors |
| dealers |
| clients |

here, …

9. It is hoped that by our joint efforts we can promote business as well as friendship. 希望通过共同努力，我们既可促进贸易又能增进友谊。

Similar structures:

It is hoped that

| on the basis of equality |
| to our mutual benefit |
| by even greater effort |
| through our endeavors |
| for our common interests |
| to the advantage of our two firms |

we can …

10．We look forward to your favorable reply. 等候佳音。

Similar structures：

We
await
appreciate
expect
anticipate
hope to receive
your favorable reply.

11．We shall be grateful if you would reply at an early date.

敬请早日答复，将不胜感激。

Similar structures：

We should be
grateful
obliged
glad
thankful
if …

We should
be appreciative of
appreciate
your early reply.

We should
be appreciative of
appreciate
it if …

It will be appreciated if …

12．Your early reply will be highly appreciated.

如蒙早日答复，将不胜感激。

Similar structures：

Your
prompt attention
immediate response
favorable reply
further instructions
wholehearted cooperation
will be greatly appreciated.

13. We visited your stand at the Guangzhou Fair and are now writing you to inquire about your green tea.

我们参观了你方设在广交会上的展位，现特致函向你方询问有关绿茶的情况。

Similar structures：

We visited your stand at the

Guangzhou Fair
Paris Trade Exhibition
Los Angeles International Fair
World Expo 2006
New York World's Fair

and are now writing to you to inquire about your products.

14. We are interested in your men's shirts displayed in your show room.

我们对你方货品展览室里陈列的男式衬衫很感兴趣。

Similar structures：

We are

interested in
in the market for
sourcing in the market
potential buyers of
a prospective importer of
considering buying
ready to purchase

your men's shirts.

15. Your advertisement in this month's issue of China Foreign Trade interests us，and we should like to receive full details of your commodities.

我们对你方在本月《中国对外贸易》上所刊登的广告很感兴趣，现请告诉该商品的详细情况。

Similar structures：

Your advertisement in this month's issue of China Foreign Trade

| commodities. |
| products. |
| lines. |
| articles. |
| merchandise. |
| goods. |
| items. |
| manufactures. |

interests us and we should like to receive full details of the

16．Please send us 5 copies of your latest catalogs at your earliest convenience.

请尽早寄来 5 份最新目录。

Similar structures：

	send	
Please	forward submit dispatch	your illustrated catalogs and mail the latest pricelist
	furnish	

to us at your earliest convenience.

17．Perhaps at the same time you could quote us your lowest prices for the above-mentioned goods.

也许与此同时你方能向我们提供上述商品的最低价。

Similar structures：

| | lowest | |
| Perhaps at the same time you could quote us your | best keenest rock-bottom prevailing competitive | prices |

for the said commodities.

18. We should also like to know your terms of payment.

我们还想了解你方各类商品的支付条件。

We should also like to know your	terms of payment. terms of business. terms and conditions. discount terms. trade terms.

19. Your products are of great interest to one of our clients in Tianjin, who wishes to have your quotations for the items specified below.

我们一位天津的客户对你方的产品很感兴趣，并盼按下列项目报价。

Similar structures：

Your products are of great interest to one of our clients in Tianjin，who

wishes to have your	quotations samples bulletin price-list price-schedule illustrated catalogs	for the items specified below.

20. If terms and delivery date are satisfactory, we should expect to place regular orders with you.

如果交易条件和交货日期合意的话，相信我们会向你方订货。

Similar structures：

If terms and delivery date are satisfactory，we should expect to place

regular trial large big considerable substantial	orders with you

> ➤ **E-commerce Dialogue**

广州蓝尔迪塑料制品有限公司外贸员 Leo 与澳洲客户 Cathy 的在线聊天记录，商议建立贸易关系以及产品（Swimming Pool Cover & Liner）简介。

Leo（Seller）：

Hello Landy，this is Leo from **Landy（Guangzhou）Plastic Products Co. , Ltd.**

We specialize in high-quality swimming pool covers and liners. I came across your company in Australia and thought our products might be of interest to you.

Cathy（Buyer）：

Hi Leo，thanks for reaching out. Yes，we're always on the lookout for good suppliers for our pool supplies. Can you give me a brief overview of your products?

Leo（Seller）：

Certainly! Our Swimming Pool Covers are designed to keep your pool clean and conserve energy. They're made from durable materials that can withstand harsh weather conditions. And our Liners come in a variety of colors and styles to match your pool's aesthetic.

Cathy（Buyer）：

That sounds promising. Do you have any specific models that are popular in Australia?

Leo（Seller）：

Yes，our Solar Max Pool Covers have been quite popular among our Australian clients due to their excellent heat retention capabilities. As for liners，our Aqua Gloss series is known for its durability and ease of installation.

Cathy（Buyer）:

I'd like to see some samples and pricing information. Can you send that to me？

Leo（Seller）:

Absolutely，I'll send you a sample package along with our latest price list. It should arrive within a week.

Cathy（Buyer）:

Great，thanks Leo. I'll review the samples and pricing，then get back to you.

Leo（Seller）:

No problem. If you have any questions or need further assistance，please don't hesitate to catch me.

Cathy（Buyer）:

Thanks for your help，Leo. I appreciate it.

Leo（Seller）:

You're welcome. I'm looking forward to hear from you. Have a good day！

Cathy（Buyer）:

You too，Leo. Cheers！

➤ **Foreign Trade Elite Literacy**

跨境电商出口增长 助力我国产品通达全球

中央经济工作会议提出，"要加快培育外贸新动能，巩固外贸外资基本盘，拓展中间品贸易、服务贸易、数字贸易、跨境电商出口。"近年来，跨境电商作为发展速度最快、潜力最大、带动作用最强的外贸新业态，显示出巨大的市场活力和增长韧性，成为外贸领域的一抹新亮色。

据海关测算，2023 年，我国跨境电商进出口总额 2.38 万亿元，增长 15.6%。其中，出口 1.83 万亿元，增长 19.6%；进口 5483 亿元，增长 3.9%。跨境电商快速发展，既满足了国内消费者多样化个性化需求，又助力我国产品通达全球，成为外贸发展的重要动能。

跨境电商依托灵活、高效、韧性的供应链，给全球贸易增长注入新动力

夜幕降临，广东广州市白云国际机场综合保税区（南区）的跨境电商企业仓库灯火通明，仓库内，成千上万的跨境电商出口商品按订单进行打包，办结海关手续后，很快将被运往机场，搭乘国际航班送到世界各地消费者手中。

随着全球化深入发展，越来越多的我国企业将目光投向海外市场，寻求更大发展空间，跨境电商出口正是其中一条重要路径。

2023 年，国务院办公厅印发《关于推动外贸稳规模优结构的意见》提出，"推动跨境电商健康持续创新发展""鼓励各地方结合产业和禀赋优势，创新建设跨境电商综合试验区，积极发展'跨境电商＋产业带'模式，带动跨境电商企业对企业出口"。

商务部国际贸易经济合作研究院副研究员朱思翘认为，在全球贸易不确定性增长和贸易低迷的情况下，跨境电商依托灵活、高效、韧性的供应链，为全球消费者提供更加物有所值的产品，也给全球贸易增长注入了新的动力。

2023 年，相关部门持续完善通关、税收、外汇等政策，创新监管模式，推动企业降本增效；支持跨境电商综试区、行业组织和企业等积极参与"丝路电商"、共建"一带一路"经贸合作，助力跨境电商出口行稳致远。

广州海关结合企业需求推出"特殊区域跨境电商出口集拼"监管模式，把同一消费者订单中各类型电商商品合并成一个包裹，办理出境通关手续，促进跨境电商全天候 24 小时通关顺畅。2023 年，广州白云机场海关已累计监管出口跨境电商商品 3.46 亿票，同比增长 51.8%。

北京海关发挥首都国际机场、大兴国际机场 2 个国际航空枢纽的优势，开展跨境电商出口货物场内"连程直转"、跨场"直连互通"，实现双枢纽联动，大幅提升跨境电商出口货物的流转效率。

"通过跨境电商出口海外仓模式，我们的自主品牌成功在国外市场站稳了脚跟。"浙江杭州维丽杰旅行用品有限公司总经理吕强说："不仅发货和售后更便捷，还能通过电商平台及时收集国外消费者的使用反馈，不断优化产品。"2023年以来，维丽杰公司通过国外跨境电商平台销售自主品牌箱包超过2 000万元，同比增长超过七成。杭州海关积极探索跨境电商发展新模式、应用新场景，支持传统产业通过新业态拓宽海外市场，将跨境电商海外仓打造成国货出海的"新驿站"。

朱思翘认为，数字技术的快速发展、区域合作的推进等，都将为跨境电商发展创造更好环境。建议持续落实好已出台的各项稳外贸政策。同时，针对新形势新任务，适时推动出台新政策新举措，完善跨境电商产业链和生态链，逐步形成一系列适应和引领全球跨境电商发展的管理制度和经贸规则，进一步增强我国跨境电商国际竞争力。

带动传统制造企业和贸易企业转型，推动新业态发展

近日，山东青岛凯瑞祥国际物流有限公司出口的一批生活用品在青岛港装船发往位于境外的海外仓。

"我们积极为企业开拓跨境电商海外市场。"凯瑞祥公司总经理王霞说，去年凯瑞祥公司为80余家企业的1 000票货物申报了跨境电商出口，今年销售态势依旧火热。

山东立足产业基础优势，创新实施"跨境电商＋产业带"培育工程，让更多本土优质产品扬帆出海。据青岛海关统计，2023年前11个月，山东包括跨境电商在内的外贸新业态进出口2 604.8亿元。

跨境电商链接不同产业，从服装、鞋帽、母婴产品到家具、家电等大件小件，各行各业都可以通过跨境电商链接到全球市场当中。同时，跨境电商带动传统制造企业和贸易企业转型，推动了新业态发展。

在位于山东济宁高新区的中国农创港（济宁）跨境电商产业园，来自金乡县的大蒜获得外国客商青睐，山东炯心贸易有限公司签下了1.2万美元的大蒜订单。"入驻产业园发展跨境电商后，订单利润率比之前提高了50%。"

炯心公司总经理韩炬说。

在上海，147 件跨境电商出口包裹近日经上海海关所属青浦海关办理完GPS 转关监管手续后，从上海青浦综合保税区运往上海浦东国际机场，将通过货运航班运往国外，直接投递至境外消费者手中。青浦海关与浦东国际机场海关通力合作，进一步优化监管模式。目前，上海青浦区已吸引 9 家全国或区域快递企业总部入驻，在青浦西片区已经初步形成跨境电商出口产业集群区。

在广东珠海，拱北海关积极助力构建大湾区跨境物流快速通道，支持符合条件的出口商品采用"简化申报、清单核放、汇总统计"方式办理报关手续，探索海陆空联运新线路，已吸引顺丰、DHL、菜鸟等多家企业在港珠澳大桥珠海公路口岸开展电商业务，出口目的地达 200 多个国家和地区。

优化监管制度，释放跨境电商贸易新活力

近日，在广州南沙综合保税区企业仓库内，数千件因尺码选购不匹配等原因退货的出口跨境电商服饰重新理货上线，在跨境电商平台被不同区域的海外消费者重新选购后，这些出口退货商品和新售商品一起"合包"发往广州白云国际机场，随后发往海外市场。

随着跨境电商快速发展，中国生产的潮流服装、服饰箱包等"快时尚"零售商品在线订货消费模式广受海外消费者青睐，但由于快消品选购存在一定的退换货率，跨境购买"退货难"问题一度成为困扰消费者和跨境出口企业的难题。

南京海关所属苏州海关针对跨境零售出海商品高客单价、迭代更新快等特点，全流程提供一站式服务，优化监管制度，建立高效、安全、便捷的通道，解决出口企业痛点，实现跨境电商商品出得去、退得回，释放跨境电商贸易新活力。

广州海关创新跨境电商出口退货一站式监管服务模式，允许企业将境外满足二次销售条件的出口电商退货商品退回南沙综合保税区，在综保区仓库内一站式完成拆包、分拣、上架、存储、复出口等业务，解决跨境电商出口退货的难点、痛点。2023 年，广州海关开展跨境电商出口退货项目申报一线退货货值超 2.4 亿美元，"合包"出口包裹超 3 100 万个。

"此前，为满足消费者退货需求，我们需要在中东、欧洲、美洲等地设置海外退货仓，成本高。如今，在海关监管服务的新模式下，可以根据实际订单将跨境电商出口包裹与退货包裹'合包'配送，节省大量物流成本和在海外设仓的仓储及管理费用。"广州市品成物流有限公司总经理马继芳说。

海关总署相关负责人表示，将扎实推进跨境电商综试区建设，持续推进市场采购贸易方式创新发展，推动跨境电商与其他业态联动互促、融合发展，不断拓宽贸易渠道，实现内外贸一体化发展，助力外贸保稳提质。

7 Practice

❶ **Complete thc Following Sentences in English.**

1. Whenever you are in the market for the products，＿＿＿＿＿＿
＿＿＿＿＿＿（请就你方的需求直接与我方联系）.

2. ＿＿＿＿＿＿＿＿＿（如果你方价格有竞争力），we are willing to place our first order for 1,200 dozen，i. e. 400 dozen of each type.

3. Only the goods which are fine in quality but low in price＿＿＿＿＿
＿＿＿＿（才能吸引我方客户）.

4. Several of our customers have recently expressed interest in your products and ＿＿＿＿＿＿＿＿＿＿（现随函附上我方有关一千辆童车的询盘）.

5. We should be obliged ＿＿＿＿＿＿＿＿＿＿＿＿
＿＿＿＿＿（如蒙报给最低成本加运费、保险费美国纽约价）for the following goods.

6. We note ＿＿＿＿＿ your letter ＿＿＿＿＿ October 5 that you are interested ＿＿＿＿＿ Chinese Cotton Piece Goods.

7．The letter we sent last week is an inquiry _____ color TV sets.

8．We produce decorative fabrics _____ different kinds.

9．We would like to know something _____ the styles prevailing _____ your end.

10．We should be pleased to send you some samples of our shoes and hats on approval _____ our own expense.

❷ **Translate the Following Letter into English.**

_____先生：

"强力"牌磁化杯(STRONG) Magnetic Cup

我们在巴黎的联合公司欲购5 000只你方天津生产的上述"强力"牌磁化杯（商品目录编号2369）。

请告知你方交易条件，天津港离岸价，包括折扣条件和交货期。如果是这种强化杯畅销的话，我们很可能为我方在欧洲的其他分公司订货。

XX 谨上

❸ Translate the Following Inquiry into Chinese.

Dear Sirs,

As it is our intention to add a comprehensive carpet section to each of our fifteen branches, hitherto we have only stocked a limited range in the furnishing departments. We have decided to approach the principal manufacturers and select the best lines available at the most competitive price.

We should be obliged if you would send us details of the various types of carpets that you have in production at the moment, together with price-lists and terms for bulk buying.

As soon as we examined your catalogs, we shall contact you to arrange a visit to your warehouse in order to inspect the carpets, choose what we require and discuss terms.

Yours faithfully

❹ Writing Practice

Messrs. Arthur Grey & Son write to China National Import & Export Corporation, stating that they have an order to supply a hotel with table-cloths. They request samples in handsome designs of medium and best linen suitable for the purpose.

新编外贸函电

Module 3　Business Negotiations

①　Learning Objectives

微课：报盘与还盘

Upon completion of this module，you should be able to：

- understand and be able to write quotation letters，firm offer & Non-firm offer letters；
- be familiar with counter-offer strategies and be able to write counter-offer letters.

②　Warm-up Questions

- Question 1：What is the fundamental difference between an offer and a counter-offer in business negotiations?
- Question 2：How do offers and counter-offers drive the negotiation process forward?
- Question 3：What strategies can be employed to craft a compelling counter-offer?
- Question 4：What cultural awareness can be useful in navigating cross-cultural negotiations?

3　Background Knowledge

● **Quotations and offers are important steps of business negotiation**

A quotation is merely a notice of the price of certain goods at which the seller is willing to sell.

An offer is an expression of selling or purchasing products at a given price, generally put forth in writing. In international trade practice, known as the price quotation, it is the reply to the inquiry's requests, and sometimes, directly to the other side without any inquiry.

● **The difference between an offer and a quotation**

A quotation is not an "offer" in the legal sense. It is just an indication of price without contractual obligation and is subject to change without previous notice.

● **The main types of an offer**

An offer can be divided into two main types: firm and non-firm offer.

A firm offer is also called an offer with engagement offer and a non-firm offer is an offer without engagement. A firm offer is a letter in which the offerer expresses a definite intention of doing business under the mentioned conditions and cannot be fallen off after being accepted. It is legally binding on the offerer in the stated period of validity.

A non-firm offer is made by means of sending catalogs, price lists, and quotations, so the main ideas about these points are conveyed. It can be considered as an inducement to business. It is related some uncertain statements. Generally, a non-firm offer is expressed in a very vague way, such as "middle (price range)", "quantity may not be too much", etc. The main terms and conditions of business, like delivery, quality, quantity, price terms, and payment are not complete. Even in some complete offers, the offerer may tell the offeree to receive the catalogs, price lists, quotations, or some pamphlets about products, and also list quotations clearly in the offer. Conditions such as "subject to our final confirmation", "I shall not sell the goods before (a certain date)" and "for reference only" will be mentioned as the symbols of the non-firm offer.

- **Counter Offer**

A counter-offer is virtually a partial rejection of the original offer. It also means a counter-proposal put forward by the buyer.

When an offeree receives the offer, he may show disagreement to some terms, such as price, packing, shipment or payment terms in the offer; he may make a counter-offer, i.e. virtually a partial rejection of the original offer and stating his own terms instead. Then the original offerer or seller becomes the offeree. If he also disagrees with the relative terms in the counter-offer, he may send a counter-counter-offer to the buyer. So a deal is usually concluded only after several cycles of bargaining.

④ Module-Related Correspondence

Letters Concerning Business Negotiations

➤ Quotation letters

➤ Non-firm offer & firm offer letters

➤ Counter-offer letters

⑤ Sample Letters

微课：外贸商品单价的构成　微课：外贸商品报价

Case 1

广州蓝尔迪塑料制品有限公司外贸业务员 Leo 收到了一封英国客户

Cathy 的询盘信函，询问 Swimming Pool Cover（太阳能游泳池盖）系列产品的信息，现在 Leo 初次向 Cathy 发出报价信函。

Quotation for Swimming Pool Cover

Dear Cathy，

We thank you for your letter of 8th June，enquiring for Swimming Pool Cover.

We are exporting Swimming Pool Cover of various brands among which Solar Swimming Pool Covers are the most famous ones. They are in great demand abroad and our stocks are running down quickly. They are popular not only for their light weight，but also for the reasonable prices. We are confident that once you have tried our Covers you will place repeat orders with us in large quantities.

Based on your requirement，we are quoting as follows：

Custom Size Solar Cover

Price：50—99 square meters ＄4. 31

　　　　≥100 square meters ＄3. 01

Shipping：＄172. 68/square meter

Min. order：50 square meters

Est. delivery：by Aug 7

Anti dust solar pool cover

Price：＄10. 00

Shipping：＄107. 55/square meter

Min. order：50 square meters

Est. delivery：by Aug 7

Payment Terms：By L/C at sight to be opened through a bank to be approved by the sellers.

Shipment：September，2019，provided the covering L/C reaches the sellers by the end of this year.

新编外贸函电

The above prices are understood to be on CIF Sidney basis. Please note that we do not allow any commission on our swimming pool cover. , but a discount of 3% may be allowed if the quantity for each specification is more than 1,000 square meters. The above quotation is made without engagement and is subject to our final confirmation.

Enclosed please find a copy of our illustrative catalogue which will give you all the details. We hope you will find them interesting and let us have your orders.

We look forward to your early reply.

Yours faithfully,

Leo

Leo

Common Expressions

- light weight 轻重量
- reasonable price 合理的价格
- repeat order 重复订单
- custom size 定制尺寸
- square meters 平方米
- min. order 最小订单量
- est. delivery 预计交货时间
- Payment Terms 付款条件
- L/C at sight 即期信用证
- CIF Sidney basis 成本加保险费加运费到悉尼价
- without engagement 不作保证
- illustrative catalogue 产品目录

Useful Expressions

- enquiry for 询问

- in great demand 需求量大

- stocks are running down quickly 库存迅速减少

- place repeat order 下重复订单

- based on your requirement 根据您的要求

- quoting as follows 报价如下

- be subject to 受……影响/制约

- let us have your order 请给我们订单

- We look forward to … 我们期待……

Case 2

广州蓝尔迪塑料制品有限公司外贸业务员 Leo 再次收到了一封英国客户 Cathy 的询盘信函，询问 Swimming Pool Cover 系列产品的信息，Leo 向 Cathy 发出虚盘信函。

A Non-Firm Offer for Solar Swimming Pool Covers

Dear Cathy，

Thank you for your enquiry of March 6 regarding our Solar Swimming Pool Covers.

Considering our long business relations，we would like to make you special offer as follows：

Commodity：Hot Sale Solar Above Ground Pool Cover High Quality

Specifications：Bubble Pool Cover For Any Shape of Pool

Sizes：customize

Packing：Each pair in a poly bag，two dozens to an enforced carton

Quantity：Min. order：50 square meters

Price：$ 3.01 — $ 4.31

continued

Shipment：April/May 2020

Payment：by Confirmed Irrevocable L/C payable at sight

This offer is subject to our final confirmation.

We await your reply in cable.

Yours faithfully，

Leo

Leo

Common Expressions

- business relations 业务关系

- special offer 特别优惠

- customize 定制

- confirmed irrevocable L/C 已确认的不可撤销信用证

- payable at sight 即期付款

Useful Expressions

- hot sale 热销

- high quality 高质量

- specifications 规格

- any shape of pool 任何形状的游泳池

- each pair in a poly bag 每对放在一个聚乙烯袋中

- two dozens to an enforced carton 两打装一个加固纸箱

- This offer is subject to our final confirmation 此报价以我方最终确认为准

Case 3

广州蓝尔迪塑料制品有限公司外贸业务员 Leo 再次收到了英国客户 Cathy 的询盘信函，询问 Solar Swimming Pool Cover 系列产品 2 款产品的信息，Leo 向 Cathy 发出实盘信函。

A Firm Offer for Solar Swimming Pool Covers

Dear Cathy，

Thank you for your enquiry of March 22，and we take pleasure in quoting the price as shown in the following firm offer delivered today subject to acceptance by 5 pm on the 5th of this April.

Please note this offer is firm. We are unable to entertain any counter offer. We quote as follows：

Commodity：Hot Sale Solar Above Ground Pool Cover

Specifications：Bubble Pool Cover for Any shape of pool

Sizes：customize

Packing：Each pair in a poly bag，two dozens to an enforced carton

Quantity：Min. order：50 square meters

Price：$ 3. 01 — $ 4. 31

Payment：by Confirmed Irrevocable L/C Payable at sight

Shipment：within 2 weeks of receiving order

With the approach of the rain season，there has been an increasing demand for high quality Solar Swimming Pool Covers.

As regards Solar Swimming Pool Covers，it is not only lightweight but crease-less on its inside surface because of special treatment. Solar Swimming Pool Covers are made from very best quality material and can be supplied in a range of designs and colors wide enough to meet the requirements of a fashionable trade such as yours.

We trust you will take advantage of this seasonal opportunity and favor us with an early reply.

Yours faithfully,

Leo

Leo

Common Expressions

- firm offer 实盘报价

- special treatment 特殊处理

- quality material 高质量材料

- fashionable trade 时尚贸易

- seasonal opportunity 季节性机会

Useful Expressions

- subject to 以……为条件

- entertain any counter offer 接受任何还价

- in a range of 在一系列中

- meet the requirements of 满足……的要求

- favor us with 惠赐（常用于请求对方给予回复或帮助）

- take advantage of 利用

- within ... of ... 在……的……之内（如：在收到订单的两周内装运）

Case 4

广州蓝尔迪塑料制品有限公司外贸业务员 Leo 发出报实盘信函后收到了英国客户 Cathy 的还盘信，希望蓝 微课：还盘信函撰写 尔迪公司的 Solar Swimming Pool Covers 产品能够降价销售，Leo 以卖家的身份向买家 Cathy 发出还盘信函。

Sellers' Counter Offer

Dear Cathy，

In reply to your letter of June 8 requesting a 7% allowance，we regret we find it very difficult to comply with.

You say you can get Solar Swimming Pool Covers of the same quality at much lower prices，but we are sure that our products are far superior in quality to any other Covers of the same price level. In actuality，the prices we quoted are closely calculated. Thanks to the high quality，considerable business has been done with many customers in other markets at these prices. You will be convinced of the reasonableness of our offer through a fair comparison of quality between our products and similar products from other sources. Therefore，considering the quality of the goods offered we do not feel that the prices we quoted are at all excessive，but bearing in mind the special character of your trade and the good and longstanding business relations between us，we have decided to offer you a special discount of 3% on an order amounting to $10,000 or over.

If you find our proposal acceptable，please let us have your order at an early date. We assure you that we always do our utmost to execute your order to your complete satisfaction.

Yours faithfully，

Leo

Leo

Common Expressions

- allowance 折扣
- price level 价格水平
- comparison 比较

77

- discount 折扣

- execute 执行

Useful Expressions

- in reply to 回复

- comply with 遵守/符合

- be superior to 优于

- in actuality 实际上

- bearing in mind 考虑到

- longstanding 长期存在的

- let us have 让我们收到

- at an early date 尽早

- do our utmost 尽我们所能

- to your complete satisfaction 令您完全满意

Writing Tips

- **Structure of Quotations and Offer Letters：**

➢ Open the letter by expressing thanks for the inquiry, if any.

➢ Explain the details of business conditions, such as name of commodities, quality, quantity, specifications, unit price, type of currency, packing condition, date of delivery, terms of payment, discount, etc.

➢ End the letter in the way that encourages the inquirers to place an order or give an early reply.

- **A Firm Offer Can be Developed in the Following Way：**

➢ Express thanks for the inquiry, if any.

➢ Explain detailed business terms: supply all the information requested including name of commodities, quality, quantity, and specifications; commissions, or discounts, if any; indicate packing and date of delivery; state clearly the validity of the offer.

➢ End the letter by asking for an early reply or expressing willingness to do business.

● **A Non-Firm Offer Can Be Developed in the Following Way**：

➢ Open the letter by expressing thanks for the inquiry，if any.

➢ Provide details of quantity，quality，price，discount，payment，packing and so on.

➢ Express the hope for a favorable reply.

● **Structure of Counter-offer Letter**：

➢ Thank the seller for the offer，mention briefly the content of the offer.

➢ Express regret at inability to accept (give the reasons for non-acceptance).

➢ Make a counter-offer，under the circumstances，it is appropriate.

➢ Hope the counter-offer will be accepted and there may be an opportunity to do business together.

6 Field Exploring

➢ **Supplementing Useful Sentences**

1. You are kindly requested to make us an offer on CIF Xiamen basis for the commodities we inquire hereunder.

敬请按我们下面所询商品以厦门到岸价报盘。

Similar structures：

You are kindly requested to

| make |
| wire |
| fax |
| telex |
| send |
| cable |
| E-mail |

us an offer for the commodities

we have listed below.

2. Thank you for your recent fax telling us that there is a good demand for our KONKA televisions in your market. We are pleased to offer them as follows.

感谢你方最近的传真——得知我方康佳电视机在你地市场有较大需求，现十分高兴地为你方报盘如下。

Similar structures：

Thank you for your recent

| facsimile |
| letter |
| cable |
| telex |
| inquiry |
| E-mail |

asking for the prices of your new

products.

We note from your recent fax that there is a good demand for our

| embroidered slippers |
| bicycle parts |
| leather boots |
| sewing machines |
| electric fans |

in your market.

3. You are kindly advised that we are sending you a special offer for the following goods in the hope that you will introduce them to prospective buyers at your end.

我们将向你方开下述商品的特惠报盘，并希望你们介绍给你方未来的买主。

Similar structures：

We are sending you this special offer

| hoping |
| in the hope |

that you will introduce

them to the prospective buyers at your end.

4. This offer is open until March 3. 此盘有效期至 3 月 3 日为止。

Similar structures：

This offer will remain

open
effective
valid
firm
available
good

until March 3.

5. We confirm having cabled you a firm offer subject to your reply reaching us by October 23.

现确认已向你方电开实盘，10 月 23 日复到有效。

Similar structures：

We confirm having cabled you a firm offer subject to

your reply reaching us
your acceptance（being）received here
our receiving your confirmation
your reply here

by November 29.

6. We confirm having cabled you a firm offer for the following goods，subject to your reply reaching us by September 20.

确认已向电报下列商品实盘，以 9 月 20 日前复到有效。

7. We offer you firm subject to your reply here within one week from today.

兹报实盘，以自本日起一周之内你方复到为准。

8. We make you an offer subject to the goods being unsold.

我方向你方报盘，以未售出为准。

9. We submit you this offer subject to prior sale.

我方向你方报盘，以先售为条件。

10. This offer is subject to your reply reaching here before the end of this month.

该报盘以你方回复本月底前到达我地为有效。

11. To develop trade between us, we trust that you would allow us a higher rate of discount.

为了促进我们之间的贸易，望能给我们更优惠的折扣。

Similar structures:

To step up trade
To encourage business
To initiate business
To promote trade
To expand business
To develop trade

between us, we trust you would allow us a

higher rate of discount.

12. Since this is our first transaction with you, we decide, as an exception, to cut the price by 2%.

鉴于这是初次交易，我们决定破例降价 2%。

Similar structures:

Since this is our initial transaction with you, we decide, as an exception,

to | cut / reduce / shade | the price by 10%.

Since this is our initial transaction with you, we decide, as an exception,

to | deduct 10% / make a reduction of 10% | from the price.

Since this is our initial transaction with you, we decide, as an exception, to offer you 10% off.

13. This is the most reasonable price we can offer at present，and any further reduction on our side is out of the question.

此系我方目前所能提供的最惠价，不能再降价。

Similar structures：

This is the most reasonable price we can offer at present，and any

further | reduction
discount
concession
compromise
deduction | on our side is out of the question.

14. We cannot entertain business even if we meet you halfway.

即使各让一半，我们仍不能与你方成交。

Similar structures：

We cannot | entertain business
accept your counter-offer
entertain your proposal
consider your suggestion
trade at your price | even if we meet you halfway.

We are not in a position to do business at your price，since it is

far below our cost price.

below our level.

too severe.

prohibitive.

too high.

quite out of line with the inter national market.

on the high side.

15. You would benefit by ordering now，as there is every indication that the prices are rising.

现在订货，对你方有利，因为一切迹象表明价格在上涨。

Similar structures：

You would benefit by ordering now，as

> there is every indication that the prices are rising.
> there is a possibility of an up creep next week.
> there is a rising tendency in the market now.
> there will be an immediate price increase soon.
> the cost of materials is steadily rising this week.
> we are expecting a 2％ rise in the price next week.
> the prices are surely going up in the near future.
> the market is firm with an upward tendency.
> the prices are on a rapid increase.

16. According to our investigation, the market is now showing a decline，so we are expecting an adjustment of the price at the end of this month.

根据我们的调查，行市超淡，因此估计价格在本月底将作调整。

Similar structures：

According to our investigation，we believe the prices are

> declining
> on the decline
> showing a decline　now.
> surely falling
> dropping

17. We have shown some flexibility in price negotiation in order to make the conclusion of business possible.

为了达成交易，我们在谈价格时已做出某些让步。

Similar structures：

The protracted negotiation and your final concession have enabled us

to | make the conclusion of business possible.
conclude the business with you.
make it possible for us to close this deal.
finalize this order with you.
succeed in securing the transaction.
come to terms at last.
reach an agreement in the end.

18. If our offer is not acceptable, please fax your best counter-offer.

如果不能接受我方报盘，请发传真告知你方最好的还盘。

19. The price you counter-offered is unreasonable.

你方还盘价格不合理。

20. To meet your request, we are prepared to reduce our freight by 3%.

为满足你方要求，我方准备将运费降低百分之三。

21. If you could make some concessions, say a reduction of 10%, we may conclude the transaction.

如果你能让步，比方说10%，我们也许能达成交易。

22. We won't make any concessions, for we will not make any profits at the price you named.

我们不能让步，因为以你们指定的价格我们将无利可图。

23. Our offer is reasonable and realistic. It comes in line with the prevailing market.

我方的报价是合理的、现实的，符合当前市场的价格水平。

24. If you insist on your price and refuse to make any concession, there will be not much point in further discussion.

如果你方坚持自己的价格，不作让步，我们没有必要再谈下去了。

25. We make a counter-offer to you of ＄150 per metric ton F. O. B. London.

我们还价为每公吨伦敦离岸价 150 美元。

26. We can't accept your offer unless the price is reduced by 5％.

除非你们减价 5％，否则我们无法接受报盘。

➢ **E-commerce Dialogue**

广州蓝尔迪塑料制品有限公司外贸业务员 Leo 与澳洲客户 Cathy 的报盘对话。

Leo：Good morning，Cathy！I hope this message finds you well.

Cathy：Good morning，Leo！Yes，I'm doing great. How can I assist you today?

Leo：I'm delighted to hear that. Cathy，I wanted to follow up on our previous discussion about Solar Pool Liners. I've prepared a firm offer for you to your requirements.

Cathy：Please go ahead and share the details.

Leo：OK！We're offering you our premium Solar Pool Liner made with high-quality PVC material. The size you requested，15m×7m，is available in stock.

Cathy：That's exactly what I'm looking for. What's the price per unit，including shipping to Australia?

Leo：We can offer you a price of AUD 2,500 per unit，with shipping included via sea freight，about 4-6 weeks to arrive. This is a firm offer valid for 10 days from today.

Cathy：That seems reasonable.

Leo：We provide a comprehensive 5-year warranty on our Solar Pool Liners.

Cathy：That's good. I'll need to run this by my team. Can you send me the detailed specifications and payment terms via E-mail?

Leo：Absolutely，Cathy. I'll draft an E-mail with all the necessary information. I'll send it over to you within the hour.

Cathy：Thank you，Leo. I appreciate your promptness and detailed offer. I'll get back to you as soon as possible.

Leo：You're welcome，Cathy. Don't hesitate to reach out if you have any further questions. Have a great day!

Cathy：Same to you，Leo. Thanks again.

➤ **Foreign Trade Elite Literacy**
外贸精英是如何提高订单转化率的？
一、分析目标市场及目标客户

盲目开发客户的成功率并不高，许多人喜欢以大范围撒网的方式去开发客户，这样的转化率往往很低。要想开发好客户，提高订单转化率，首要前提条件就是了解你的客户。

我们要养成分析客户的习惯，分析客户是指要分析客户的采购产品、交易次数、交易重量、采购行为、采购记录、客户合作过的供应商明细和竞争对手分析等相关的贸易明细记录，这些是我们了解客户的重要参考。

那么，这些参考数据和记录从哪里来呢？我们可以从海关数据网站、谷歌、脸书和领英等搜索引擎和社交网站找到产品关键词、客户公司名、联系人名称，以及竞争对手公司、联系人名称等信息。然后筛选你挖掘得来的信息，将这些信息分门别类地记录下来。整理好客户信息，对以后的订单跟进将非常便利。

另外一点值得注意的是，信息每天都在更新，这些信息具有一定的时效性。因此，我们需要将每次更新的数据情况记录好，避免下次更新时做重复的工作。这样既能节省时间，又能很清楚自己每项工作的进度。

二、对客户实行不同的价格吸引策略

无论是涨价还是降价，都是为了吸引客户。通过对客户的分析和预估，了解到客户的需求，我们就能通过不同的定价、涨价、降价等方式去吸引客户，实现成交。

1. 涨价如何吸引客户

涨价不仅仅是表面上的价格上浮。股票市场上的"买涨不买跌"的心理同样可以运用到贸易市场，我们涨价的目的不是为了提高利润，而是为了告诉客户整体市场的价格波动走向是向上的，如果现在不买，后面价格还要涨，这样能够尽快促成客户成交。实际上，客户还是选择了"相对便宜"的价格。

具体操作时，我们可以以原材料价格上涨为由告知客户，我们的产品价格将要向上调整；或者告知客户由于汇率波动的原因，价格将有所上升。总之，我们"准备合理地提高价格"的举动就是促成客户尽快交易的动力。

2. 降价如何吸引客户

如果说即将涨价能够更快刺激客户的购买欲望，那么已经降价就是真实地刺激客户下订单，如果能在保证质量的基础上，将商品适当地降低价格，以此来鼓励客户下单。当客户犹豫不决时，我们可以在保证质量的情况下适当地降低价格，并且以时效性去刺激客户下单——再不买就恢复原价了。

三、以成单量来展示自己的实力

大部分业务员得不到客户的信任是因为无法证明自己。他们无法证明自己可以跟好客户的订单，也无法证明公司有实力完成客户的订单，这时，我们就需要从外部"拿"一些数据来证明自己。我们可以通过公司的成单量、自己的跟单量等数据来向客户展示自己的实力。

客户其实都有一种跟风的心态。让客户看到这么多人在你这里下订单了，他也会觉得你的产品是好的、服务是好的，才有那么多人选择你，这是一种从众心理。

⑦ Practice

❶ **Complete the Following Sentences in English.**

1. As the price quoted by us is reasonable，＿＿＿＿＿＿＿＿（我们相信你方能够接受）.

2. The prices listed in our ＿＿＿＿＿＿＿＿＿＿＿＿＿＿（均为新港交货价）.

3. ＿＿＿＿＿＿＿＿＿＿＿（一旦获得进口许可证），please fax us so that we can get the goods ready.

4. ＿＿＿＿＿＿＿＿＿＿＿（这是我方最优惠的报盘），which you can not obtain elsewhere.

5. In order to promote the development of our business，＿＿＿＿＿＿ ＿＿＿＿＿＿＿＿＿＿（我们决定按大连交货价向你方报盘）.

6. Unless otherwise stated，the above offer＿＿＿＿＿＿＿（以先售为条件）.

7. Thank you for your letter of October 1 asking us to ＿＿＿＿＿＿＿（你方报盘 500 个美的牌电饭锅）for May shipment.

8. For your information，＿＿＿＿＿＿＿＿＿＿＿＿＿（我们的报价中已包含你方百分之五的佣金）.

9. As requested，we are making you an offer as follows ＿＿＿＿＿＿（每箱 84 美元 CIF 新港）.

10. The commission on our shoes would be allowed ＿＿＿＿＿＿ ＿＿＿＿＿（以不少于 1000 箱的购买量）.

❷ Translate the Following Letter into English.

敬启者：

为复你方三月二十六日询价，现报盘如下，以我方最后确认为准：

4 000 打工作手套，每打……美元新加坡成本加运费净价，规格见附页，船期八、九月。付款要求以保兑的、不可撤销的信用证凭即期汇票支付，在装船前 30 天开出。另邮寄去各种尺寸的样品以及所需要的小册子。

若觉得上述报盘可接受，请来电以便我方确认。

❸ Translate the Following Letter into Chinese.

Dear Sirs，

We have received your enquiry sheet of 1st Aug. together with the attached sample for which we thank you.

As for the result of inspection of sample，we may assure you that we are in a position to manufacture the same products in design and quality as the sample.

On the basis of 100,000 pairs annual requirement，we offer you as follows：

Price：25 cents CIF Dalian per pair

Packing：in plastic bags outer-packed in cardboard cartons.

新编外贸函电

Payment: by irrevocable confirmed sight L/C

Delivery: during Nov./Dec. 90 days after receipt of your order.

We can assure you that this price is the lowest price according to the above quantity. You may refer to our catalogue regarding the other technique items.

Please give us your directions if you have any problems.

Yours faithfully,

Encl: a copy of catalogue

④ **Writing Practice.**

Write a letter to the buyers, stating that you have plenty of the goods they need and you can offer them.

新编外贸函电

Module 4 Packing

微课：国际贸易的商品包装

① Learning Objectives

Upon completion of this module, you will:

- understand the classification and terms of packing in international trade;
- understand the buyer's requirement of packing and be able to reply to discuss packing arrangement;
- understand the buyer's requirement of shipping marks and be able to reply to discuss it.

② Warm-up Questions

- Question 1: How do people usually pack the goods in international trade?
- Question 2: How many packing containers do you know?
- Question 3: Why are the markings on the outer packing important?
- Question 4: As a salesperson, do you know how to respond to customer's requirement of packing?

3 Background Knowledge

微课：国际货运包装种类和常见标识

Packing is of great importance for most of the goods in international trade. Proper packing can not only keep the goods safe, facilitate loading, unloading and stowage, prevent loss and leakage in their whole circulation, but also promote sales. Therefore, packing terms should be negotiated by the two contractual parties and must be definitely stipulated in the contract on the part of goods which need packing.

- **Cargoes Classification**

Not all goods require packing. In international trade, from the perspective of whether packing is required, goods can be divided into the following three categories.

1）Bulk cargoes or cargoes in bulk：like wheat, mineral ore, coal, etc.

散装货物，指颗粒状、粉末状、无包装的货物，如小麦、矿物矿石，煤炭等。

2）Nude cargoes：like vehicles, bronze or steel plates or blocks.

裸装货物，如车辆、铜、钢板材或砌块等。

3）Packed cargoes：all the other cargoes.

包装货物，除上述以外其他所有货物

For the packed cargoes, they need to be packed properly before shipment, in case that they are damaged or contaminated during transportation. The packing method, or the choice of packing materials, can all be negotiated and should be agreed by both parties of transaction.

- **Two Types of Packing**

The ways of packing is decided by the type of the products and their destination, and it can be generally divided into two types: outer packing and inner packing.

1. outer packing/transportation packing 运输包装、外包装

Outer packing is used for the convenience of protecting and transporting goods. In addition, it provides easy marks for operation staff at the stocks to distinguish the goods they handle and for consignees to identify their goods when receiving them at the destination ports. The packing in the context of international trade refers mainly to this type.

2. inner packing/ packing for sales 销售包装、内包装

Inner packing is designed for the promotion of sales. It is artistically attractive, not only protect, but also prettify commodities. In this sense, inner packing can be seen as an inseparable part of the product.

● **Packing Containers Commonly Used in International Trade**

Here are some of the packing containers commonly used in international trade.

- bag 袋；包
- sack 袋子
- carton 纸板箱
- case 箱
- box 盒；箱
- crate 板条箱
- drum 铁皮圆桶（used for liquid or greasy cargoes）
- bale 包；布包
- can（or Tin）听，罐头
- keg 小圆桶
- cask 木桶
- polybag 塑料袋
- barrel 琵琶桶
- sack/gunny bag 麻袋
- bundle 捆
- container 集装箱
- pallet 托盘
- carboy 大玻璃瓶

新编外贸函电

Here are some of the packing containers commonly used in international trade.

Bag 袋；包　　Sack 袋子　　Cartib 纸板箱　　Case 箱　　Box 盒；箱　　Crate 板条箱

Drum 铁皮圆桶 (used for liquid or greasy cargoes)　　Bale 包；布包　　Can (Or Tin) 听；罐头　　Keg 小圆桶　　Cask 木桶　　Polybag 塑料袋

Barrel 琵琶桶　　Sack/gunny bag 麻袋　　Bundle 捆　　Container 集装箱　　Pallet 托盘　　Carboy 大玻璃瓶

□Bag or Sack 袋 paper/plastic/linen bags：纸/塑料/亚麻袋 It is commonly used for powder and granular（颗粒的）materials. 它通常用于粉末和颗粒状（颗粒的）材料。	
□Bale 包 The bale is used for bulky items that can be compressed. 捆包通常用于可压捆的大件物品。	
□Carton 纸板箱（CTN） The carton is widely used in export packing because it is light，resilient，cheap，and most suitable when carried within a metal container. 纸箱被广泛用于出口包装，因为它很轻，有弹性，便宜，最适合在铁皮集装箱内应用。	
□Wooden Case 木箱 The wooden case is strong. It is used for small, heavy items. 木箱很坚固，适用于小而重的物品。	

续表

☐Drum/barrel/cask 桶

It is used for carrying liquids, chemicals and paints, etc.

桶被用于运送液体、化学品和油漆等。

☐Wooden Crate 木制板条箱

This is usually used for large and heavy objects like machines, stones and animals.

木制板条箱通常用于运装大型和重型物体，如机器、石头和动物等。

☐Can/Tin 罐头，听

It is a small metal container for paint, oil or foodstuff.

指盛放油漆、油或食品的小金属容器。

☐Carboy 大玻璃瓶

It is a glass or plastic container used for chemical.

玻璃或塑料容器用于化学品运输。

☐Pallet 货盘，托盘

It is used to hold a number of packages or pieces.

托盘用于容纳一定数量的包裹或散件。

☐Container 集装箱

It is used to transport goods by road, rail, sea or air.

它用于容纳公路、铁路、海运或空运运输的货物。

• **Factors Influencing Ways of Packing**

How to pack the goods? What kind of material is the best choice? These are the questions that buyers and sellers always argue. Actually，the following factors may influence people's choice about the ways of packing.

1．Packing should be designed according to the need of the cargo.

2．Packing should be in compliance with import country's customs or statutory requirements.

3．Packing must meet insurance acceptance conditions.

4．Packing should also be economical while being sufficient，and make the handling as easy as possible.

5．Marking of the packing themselves is of equal importance.

• **Marking**

One thing closely related to packing is the packing mark，which is also called marking. Generally speaking，there are three kinds of packing marks.

1．Shipping mark：运输标志、唛头

2．Indicative mark：指示标志

3．Warning mark：警告标志

These marks can be stenciled on each side of a carton.

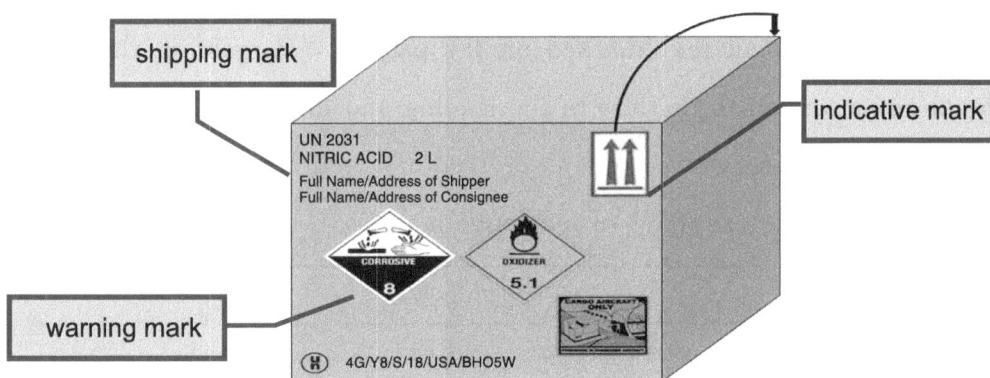

Shipping Marks 运输标志/唛头

The shipping marks are used for cargoes to be identified during transportation.

For example，this picture shows a typical triangle shipping mark. It include four parts.

1) ABC is the abbreviations of consignees or buyers.

2) New York is the name of the unloading port or destination.

3) Nos. 1-600 is the package number 600 means the total number of cases, 1 means this is the first one.

4) 234MKY-5678 is the reference number, which refers to the number of the shipping documents, such as L/C, bill of lading, invoice or contract.

Triangle-shaped shipping mark

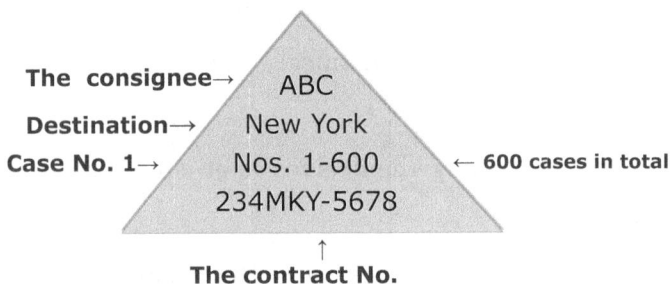

The consignee→　ABC
Destination→　New York
Case No. 1→　Nos. 1-600　← 600 cases in total
　　　234MKY-5678
↑
The contract No.

Besides these, other information of this shipment may also appear in the markings, such as weight, measurement, the place of origin, and so on.

Indicative Marks 指示标志

Indicative marks are also called handling marks, which are simple, eye-catching graphics and text marked on the packing, suggesting that people should pay attention to matters in the loading and unloading, transportation and storage process.

Here are some examples of indicative marks.

Handle with care	小心搬运
This side up	此面朝上
Don't throw down	请勿抛掷
Perishable goods	易腐物品
Not to be laid flat	请勿平放
No hooks	请勿用钩

Fragile	易碎品
Guard against Damp	防潮
Keep cool，Keep in cool place	保持冷藏
Keep out of the direct sun	避免日光直射

Handle with care 小心搬运	This side up 此面朝上	Don't throw down 请勿抛掷	Perishable goods 易腐物品	Not to be laid flat 请勿平放
小心轻放	向 上			
No hooks请勿用钩	Fragile易碎品	Guard against damp防潮	Keep cool, Keep in cool place保持冷藏	Keep out of the direct sun 避免日光直射
禁用手钩	易碎			

Warning Marks 警告性标志

Warning marks are also called dangerous marks. They are used to illustrate the commodity is flammable，explosive，or dangerous goods. These marks also use graphics and text.

Here are some examples of warning marks.

Dangerous goods	危险品
Inflammable gases/liquids/solid	可燃气体/液体/固体
Explosives	易爆品
Poison substances	有毒物品
Corrosive substances	腐蚀性物品
Radioactive substances	放射性物质

⚠	Danger Electric shock risk	⚠	Danger Compressed gas
⚠	Danger High voltage	⚠	Caution Mind the step
⚠	Danger Toxic	⚠	Caution Mind your head
⚠	Danger Harmful fumes	⚠	Caution Slippery surface
⚠	Danger Fire risk	⚠	Caution Automatic door
⚠	Danger Highly flammable material	⚠	Caution
⚠	LPG Highly flammable	⚠	Danger
⚠	Danger Flammable liquid	⚠	Caution Hot

④ Module-Related Correspondence

Letters Concerning Packing:

➤ Letters concerning packing arrangement and mark

➤ Letters concerning negotiating packing arrangement

➤ Letters concerning discussing shipping marks.

⑤ Sample Letters

微课：包装安排信函

Case 1

TIC 公司的销售小王刚刚接到美国 BOB 公司 500 件晚礼服的订单。在信中，买方提出了明确的包装要求。

Buyer's Letter to Put Forward Packing Requirement

Dear MS Wang,

We have received your quotation dated June 15 with many thanks.

Enclosed please find our order No. ASK-535 for 500 pieces of evening dresses at the price of $268 per piece CFR New York.

As this is the first transaction between us, we would like to make it clear that, according to what we have discussed before, each evening dress is to be packed in one polythene bag, then into a rigid cardboard box with ribbons, 10 boxes to a carton lined with waterproof sheet and strengthened by straps outside.

Please see to it that the cases should be strong enough to protect the goods from any possible damage in transit.

If you think this is acceptable to you, please let us know as soon as possible.

Yours sincerely,

Anna Smith

Anna Smith

Sales Manager

Common Expressions

- 表示"用某物包装，用某种形式包装"："in …"

1) Walnuts are packed in double gunny bags.

核桃用双层麻袋包装。

2）Each item is individually packed in a wooden case.

每件单独用一个木箱装。

• 表示"用某物包装，每件装多少"："in … of … each" / "in … , each containing …"

e. g.

1）The canned mushrooms are packed in wooden cases of 10 dozen each.

蘑菇罐头用木箱装，每箱 10 打。

2）The goods will be packed in iron drums of 25 kilos net（each）.

货物用铁桶装，每桶净重 25 千克。

3）Nylon socks are to be packed in cartons，each containing 50 dozen.

尼龙袜会用纸板箱包装，每箱 50 打。

4）Cement is to be packed in double craft-paper bags，each containing 50 kilos.

水泥要用双层牛皮纸包装，每袋装 50 千克。

• 表示"用某物包装，每件装多少，若干小容器装于一大容器中"："in … of … each，… to …"

e. g. Pens are packed in boxes of a dozen each，100 boxes to a wooden case.

钢笔要用盒装，每盒装一打，100 盒装于一木箱。

• 多层次包装时可用此句型："… to a …，… to a …"

1）Pens are packed in paper boxes，10 pieces to one box.

钢笔要用纸盒包装，每盒装 10 支。

2）Candles are packed 20 pieces to a paper box，40 boxes to a carton.

蜡烛每 20 支装一纸盒，40 纸盒装一纸板箱。

Case 2

小王觉得买家对包装的要求可以接受，于是回信告诉了买方这个订单的包装安排。

Seller's Reply to Packing Requirements

Dear MS Smith，

Your letter concerning packing requirements reached us the day before yesterday. We can meet your requirements and are now making arrangements accordingly.

As requested，each evening dress is packed in a polythene bag，then into a rigid cardboard box，10 boxes to a carton lined with waterproof sheet and strengthened by double straps outside.

Enclosed please find a picture of our newly designed deep purple cardboard box with a golden ribbon，and the dimensions are 20cm high，30cm wide and 50cm long. All the cartons are up to export standard and are strong enough for ocean transportation.

We trust you will find the packing satisfactory.

Yours Sincerely，

Amy Wang

Amy Wang

Encl.：a picture of the cardboard box

Common Expressions

● meet your requirements 满足你的要求

e. g. Although we are keen to meet your requirements，we regret being unable to comply with your request for a reduction in price.

虽然我方想满足你方要求，但抱歉不能按照你方要求降低价格。

• As requested 按照你的要求

e. g. As requested，we send you under cover a quotation sheet showing our lowest price for cotton.

应你方要求，我们随函附上棉花最低报价单。

• be lined with 内衬……

e. g. Each case should be lined with a waterproof sheet to avoid moisture.

每个箱子都应有防水布内衬，以防止货物受潮。

• dimension 尺寸

e. g. The dimensions of the carton are 17cm high，30cm wide and 50cm long. The volume then is about 0. 026 cubic meters.

纸板箱体积是高 17 厘米，宽 30 厘米和长 50 厘米，容积大约是 0.026 立方米。

• be up to 达到……标准

e. g. All the goods will be thoroughly examined before shipment and are up to the export standard.

所有货物在装运前都将经过彻底检查，并符合出口标准。

Useful Expressions

• Please make sure to use shockproof packing.

请务必用防震包装。

• The new packing of the porcelain is of typical Chinese style.

陶瓷的包装是典型的中国特色。

• Each case should be lined with foam plastics in order to protect the goods from pinch.

每个箱子都有内衬泡沫塑料，以便货物不受挤压。

• We require the sweaters to be packed each in one poly bag，5 dozen to a lined carton with waterproof sheet and secured by two iron straps outside.

我们要求将毛衣每件套一个塑料袋，每 5 打装一有防水衬里，外用两条铁箍绑紧的纸箱。

• Men's shirts are wrapped in poly bags each and then packed/put in a paper box，50 boxes to a moisture proof carton，2 cartons to a wooden case.

每件男士衬衫先用塑料袋裹好，然后装入纸盒，每50盒装一防潮纸箱，两纸板箱装一木箱。

● About the packing of our ordered goods，we suggest that they should be wrapped in polythene wrappers and packed in cardboard boxes padded with foam plastic，ten toy cars each，50 boxes to a wooden case lined with oil cloth.

关于包装问题，我们建议每件玩具车用聚乙烯袋装好，然后放入铺有泡沫塑料软垫的纸盒中，每盒装10辆玩具车，每50盒装入一个衬有油纸的木箱中。

● We can meet your requirements to have the goods packed in wooden cases but you have to bear the extra packing charge / the extra packing charge will be for your account.

我们可以满足您的要求，用木箱包装货物，但额外的包装费用将由您来承担。

● Taking into consideration the long distance transport，we have especially reinforced our packing.

考虑到长途运输，我们特别加强了包装。

● Our packaging is seaworthy and strong enough to stand rough handling.

我们的包装适合海运，足够牢固，经得起野蛮搬运。

● We require the inner packing to be small and exquisite to help sales and the outer packing to be light and strong to be easy to carry.

我们要求内包装小而精致，以帮助销售，外包装轻而结实，便于携带。

Writing Tips

Structure of Seller's Reply to Packing Requirements：

➢ Part 1：Acknowledge receipt of the letter of packing requirements. Notify whether or not you will comply with requested.

➢ Part 2：If you agree with the customer's request，confirm the details of the packing；If there is a disagreement，state convincing reasons.

➢ Part 3：Close the letter with a hope for a favorable reply.

Case 3

新加坡某公司欲从汕头市双丰玩具公司订购一批合金压铸模型车(玩具车)，并对于包装盒运输标志提出了一些咨询。

微课：装运唛头

Buyer's Letter to Inquire about Packing and Shipping Marks of a Certain Product

---

Dear Mr. Lin,

Thanks for your offer on Dec. 21，2024 and we are pleased to place an initial order for 1，200 your Alloy Die-cast Model Cars CT055.

Regarding to the packing of this order，we wish to draw your attention to the following matters：

As the model cars are easy to be squeezed and deformed during transportation，please see to it that the packing should be strong enough to withstand rough handling. Besides，we want the customized logo to be printed on the inner packing.

Please mark the gross weight，net weight and tare weight on the outer packing，and the words "Fragile，Handle with Care" should be stenciled on both sides of the case.

If your find the above requirement acceptable，please favor us with your reply at your earliest convenience.

Yours sincerely,

Gordon Brown

Gordon Brown

Common Expressions

- initial order 首次订单

- regarding to 关于

- squeeze 挤压

- deform 变形

- withstand 经受住、承受住

- rough handling 粗暴操作

- customized logo 客订标识

- gross weight 毛重

- net weight 净重

- tare weight 皮重

- fragile 易碎（品）

- handle with care 小心搬运

- stencil 用模板印（文字或图案），俗称"刷唛头"

e. g. The shipping marks should be stenciled on both sides of the outer packing. 装运标记应印在外包装的两侧。

- favor us with your reply at your earliest convenience 尽早回复

Case 4

汕头市双丰玩具公司的销售员杨林收到上述新加坡的客户来信后，写信回应关于商品的包装和唛头要求。

Seller's Reply to Inquiry of Packing and Shipping Marks

Dear Mr. Brown,

Re：Packing and Shipping Marks

In reply to your letter of July 16th inquiring about the packing of our Alloy Die-cast Model Cars CT055, we state the following:

新编外贸函电

Our export models cars are each packed in a cardboard box with customized logo，1 dozen to a rigid folding paper box，20 boxes to a double-wall corrugated carton lined with waterproof material and bound with PET straps outside. The cardboard box for inner packing has a clear window and the car inside can be seen directly. The dimensions of the corrugated carton are 30 cm high，20 cm wide and 40 cm long，with a volume of about 0. 024 cubic meters. The gross weight is 8. 5 kg，the net weight is 6. 5 kg.

With reference to shipping marks，in addition to the gross weight，net weight and tare weight on the outer packing，we will mark your initials WCK and the contract number in a diamond，under which the package number and port of the destination will also be stenciled. Furthermore，warning marks like HANDLE WITH CARE，KEEP DRY，etc. will also be indicated.

Should you have any special requirements in packing and shipping marks，please let us know. We will meet your requirement to the best of our ability.

Yours sincerely，

Yang Lin

Yang Lin

Common Expressions

● In reply to：兹复……，在此答复……

e. g.

1) In reply to your enquiry yesterdays，we are sending you herewith several samples of wall paper closely resembling to what you want.

针对你方昨日的询盘，现寄上与你来函要求相似的墙纸样品一宗。

2) In reply，we are offering you firm as per terms of your last order CT598 as follows.

兹复，我们按你方上次 CT598 号订单的条件报实盘如下。

- state：说明，声明

e. g.

1) We believe we have stated explicitly the importance of anti-leakage packaging.

我们认为已经清晰地向您说明了防渗漏包装的重要性。

2) Partial shipment is not allowed as stated in the L/C.

按照信用证规定，不允许分装。

- corrugated carton：瓦楞纸箱

- single-wall corrugated carton 单层瓦楞纸箱

- double-wall corrugated carton 双层瓦楞纸箱

- triple-wall corrugated carton 三层瓦楞纸箱

- be bound with：用……捆绑

e. g.　The wooden case will be bound with two iron straps to prevent it from falling apart during transportation.

木箱将用两条铁带捆扎，以防止在运输过程中散开。

- cubic meters：立方米

- square meters：平方米

- in addition to：*besides* 此除……之外

e. g.　In addition to porcelain tableware, we also have a large supply of other blue and white porcelain products, such as vases and table lamps.

除了瓷器餐具，我们还供应大量其他青花瓷产品，如花瓶和台灯。

- indicate：表明

e. g.　Information indicated that the market is rising.

有消息表明市场行情看涨。

- (do sth.) to the best of one's ability：*try one's best to do sth.* / *make every effort to do sth.* 尽某人最大的能力

e. g.　We will match the quality of the product with the sample to the best of our ability.

我们将尽最大努力使产品质量与样品相匹配。

Useful Expressions

• Each package will be marked "Fragile".

每件包装上都会标明"易碎品"。

• As required, we have stenciled "Handle with Care", and other relative marks on the cartons.

按照你方要求，我们已在外包装上刷上"小心轻放"和其他有关标记。

• We have marked all cases as per your instructions.

我方已按照你方指示给所有箱子刷唛。

• The cases are to be marked with the lot number as given in the order sheet.

箱子上会按订单所示刷上批号。

• We will mark your initials SCC in a diamond, under which the port of destination and our order number should be stenciled.

我们会刷上一菱形，内刷贵公司首字字母 SCC，下刷目的港及我方订单号。

• "Fragile, Handle with Care" will be printed on both sides of the carton.

"易碎，小心轻放"的标志会印在纸箱的两侧。

Writing Tips

Structure of Seller's Reply to：

➤ Part 1：Acknowledge the receipt of the buyer's letter.

➤ Part 2：Specify the packing arrangement.

➤ Part 3：Describe the shipping marks.

➤ Part 4：Close the letter and express willingness to meet other requirements.

6 **Field Exploring**

➢ **E-commerce Dialogue**

关于 Swimming Pool Lights 的包装

广州蓝尔迪塑料制品有限公司外贸员林与澳洲客户 Cathy 的在线聊天记录，讨论泳池灯的包装。

Cathy（Buyer）： Hello，Lin. I wish to know the details of the packing of your Swimming Pool Lights.

Lin（Seller）： No problem. Go ahead，please.

Cathy（Buyer）： How are the goods packed and packaged?

Lin（Seller）： Each in one water-proof bag，20 PCS to one box，100 boxes to a wooden case.

Cathy（Buyer）： What measures will you take to protect the goods from dampness or breakage?

Lin（Seller）： Directive marks like Keep Dry，Fragile，Handle with Care，etc. would be indicated.

Cathy（Buyer）： Sounds not bad.

Lin（Seller）： Don't worry. You should trust us that we will give special care to the packing to avoid damage in transit.

➢ **Foreign Trade Elite Literacy**

绿色包装（Green Package）

绿色包装（Green Package）又可称为环保包装（Eco-friendly Packing）、可持续包装（Sustainable Packaging）、无公害包装（Pollution-free Packaging）和环境之友包装（Environmental-friendly Packaging），指的是对生态环境和人类健康无害，能重复使用和再生，符合可持续发展原则的包装。

其理念有两个方面的含义：一是保护环境，二是节约资源。这两者相辅相成，不可分割。其中保护环境是核心，节约资源与保护环境密切相关，因为节约资源可减少废弃物，这实际上就是从源头上对环境的保护。

从技术角度看，绿色包装是指以天然植物和有关矿物质为原料研制成对生态环境和人类健康无害，有利于回收利用，易于降解，符合可持续发展要求的一种环保型包装。也就是说，其包装产品从原料选择、产品制造到使用和废弃的整个生命周期，均应符合生态环境保护的要求，实现绿色包装应从绿色包装材料、包装设计和大力发展绿色包装产业三方面入手。

绿色包装一般包含以下分类：

可回收包装（Recyclable Packaging）：由可以在传统设施中回收的材料制成。可回收是指在包装的使用寿命结束后可以进行回收处理。

消费后回收包装（Post-Consumer Recycled Packaging，PCR）：指由已经处理和回收并转化为新包装的材料制成的新包装。

可生物降解包装（Biodegradable Packaging）：通常由植物基或生物塑料材料制成，这种包装可能含有有助于分解材料的微生物。

可堆肥包装（Compostable Packaging）：由天然植物材料制成，这些材料可以自然返回地球，帮助地球系统再生。

● **绿色物流（Green Logistics）**

现代物流的快速发展伴随着大量能源消耗和对环境的负面影响。为了积极减少碳排放，绿色物流已经成为全球物流行业发展的重要趋势，也是实现可持续发展的必经之路。

绿色物流是指通过充分利用物流资源，采用先进的物流技术，合理规划和实施运输、储存、装卸、搬运、包装、流通加工、配送、信息处理等物流活动，以降低物流对环境影响的过程。（定义来源：《中华人民共和国国家标准-绿色物流指标构成与核算方法 GB/T37099-2018》）。

绿色物流是一种采用可持续发展原则、以最小化资源消耗和减少环境影响为目标的物流管理方法。它强调在物流和供应链管理中，通过改进运输、仓储和包装等方面的措施，减少资源使用和环境影响，提高效率和可持续性，实现经济效益和社会效益的双赢。

绿色物流的业务构成主要包括以下几个方面。

绿色运输：指为了降低物流活动中的交通拥挤、污染等带来的损失，促进社会公平、节省建设维护费用，从而发展低污染、有利于环境的多元化交通工具，来完成物流活动的协和交通运输系统，以及最大限度地降低交通污染程度，而采取的对交通源、交通量、交通流的规制体系。

绿色仓储：指采用节能、环保、安全、智能化等技术和管理手段，减少对环境和人体健康的影响，提高资源利用效率，促进可持续发展的仓储系统。

绿色装卸：指以低能耗、低污染、低碳排放为目标，通过采用新技术、新设备和新方法，实现减少装卸活动对环境的负面影响。同时，可以优化作业流程，提高运作效率和质量，降低运营成本，保障作业安全的一种装卸方式。

绿色搬运：指利用绿色技术、能源、装备和管理等手段，改变搬运方式和流程，实现节能减排、低碳环保、高效运作的搬运方式。

绿色包装：指在产品包装的设计、制造、使用和处理过程中，采用环保材料、技术和方式，以减少资源消耗、能源消耗和废弃物产生为目的，尽可能减少对环境的负面影响，保护生态系统，促进可持续发展同时提高经济效益和社会责任感的一种可持续发展的包装方式。

绿色流通加工：指物品在从生产地到使用地过程中，根据需要对包装、分割、计量、分拣、组装、价格贴付、标签贴付、商品检验等简单作业，采用各种节能环保技术和措施，减少对环境的影响和污染，提高资源利用效率，促进可持续发展的一种流通加工方式。

绿色配送：指在物流过程中，采用可持续和环保的方式和技术手段，减少对环境造成的不良影响，通过选择合理运输路线，有效利用车辆，科学配装，提高运输效率，降低物流成本和资源消耗，实现对配送环境的净化，使配送资源得到最充分利用。

信息处理绿色化：指通过数字化、环保、智能技术等手段实现物流信息高效管理，提升物流效率，减轻物流行业对环境的影响。其措施包括但不限于：建立基于互联网和物联网技术的物流信息管理平台，集成网络运输订单、物料库存信息、交通路况、天气预报等数据，并实现数据共享。

⑦ Practice

❶ Fill in the Blanks with Proper Words.

1）We should pack the goods _____ rigid boxes as you recommended.

2）Each case should be lined _____ a waterproof sheet to avoid moisture.

3）We have especially reinforced our packing in order to minimize the extent of any possible damage _____ the table wares.

4）We require each smartwatch to be put in a polythene bag to ensure protection _____ dampness.

5）To avoid pilferage，we hope that the goods will be packed in wooden cases _____in cartons as the cartons are easier to be cut open.

6）We suggest that this table lamp _____ packed each _____ a triple-wall corrugated carton measuring 3×3×2 feet，a dozen _____ one wooden case.

7）The goods are to be packed _____ wooden cases，fastened _____ iron straps outside.

8）The buyer suggested that the packing of this article _____ improved.

9）Our toy cars are customarily packed _____ standard boxes _____ one dozen each，50 boxes _____ a carton.

10) The indicative mark Keep Cool should be stenciled _____ both sides of the carton.

❷ Translate the Following Sentences into Chinese.

1) About the packing of our ordered goods, we suggest that they should be wrapped in polythene wrapper and packed in cardboard boxes padded with foam plastic, ten toy cars each, 50 boxes to a wooden case lined with oil cloth.

_____

_____

2) Our containers are in complete conformity to the specification laid down by the International Standardization Organization.

_____

_____

3) Our cartons for canned food are not only sea-worthy, but also strong enough to protect the goods from damage.

_____

_____

4) We assure you that the LED lights will be packed in a manner which facilitates their handling in transit and ensures their safe arrival at your port.

_____

_____

5) As crystal chandeliers are fragile, please make sure you pack them in strict accordance with our instructions.

_____

_____

❸ **Translate the Following Sentences into English.**

1)12 支圆珠笔装一盒，200 盒装一个纸箱。

_____

_____

2)我们要求将毛衣每件套一个塑料袋，每 5 打装一有防水衬里，外用两条铁箍绑紧的纸箱。

_____

_____

3)每件男士衬衫先用塑料袋裹好，然后装入纸盒，每 50 盒装一防潮纸箱，两纸板箱装一木箱。

_____

_____

4)我们已收到你方关于 500 打亚麻桌布的包装要求。

_____

_____

5)女士运动鞋每双装一纸盒，12 盒装一纸箱，大、中、小号平均搭配。

_____

_____

6)请放心，我们的双层瓦楞纸箱符合中国出口标准。

_____

_____

7)请注意，箱子上标有"易碎"或"小心轻放"字样，目的港、包装号、毛重和净重、尺寸和唛头应印在每个包装上。

_____

_____

8)箱子的尺寸长 1.3 米，宽 1.5 米，高 1.7 米，体积约为 3.315 立方米。总重量是 47.8 千克。

_____

_____

9)为了防止运输中的可能发生的货损，我们请求贵方采用带有防水内里的结实小巧的木盒包装。

_____

_____

10)为了方便搬运和节省运费，从下批订单开始，我方将使用纸箱包装代替原来的木箱包装。

_____

_____

❹ **Translate the Following Letter into English.**

敬启者：

感谢贵方 2024 年 6 月 1 日的来信，询问 C96-A7 订单项下的中式餐具的包装事宜。今致函，确认该商品包装方式如下。

1. 每套餐具采用三层瓦楞纸箱包装，一套一箱。同时箱子内垫有塑料泡沫以免货物受压和碰撞。

2. 外包装上使用菱形，内刷上贵公司的名称缩写 WOK，以及目的港、件数和订单号。此外，还用三角形标明"易碎""勿压"等指示性用语。

请相信我们会在包装前对货物进行彻底检查，以确保货物安全抵达你地，并令你满意。

×××谨上

新
编
外
贸
函
电

⑤ Writing Practice

美国 EMC Company 打算从广州慧采公司进口一批丝绸绣花旗袍（silk embroidered cheongsam）。由于高档旗袍的包装要求比较严格，慧采公司的业务员 Amy 写信向客户回复该商品的包装事宜。

1. 根据客户建议，已改进旗袍的内包装，拟将原来的普通纸盒改为有紫色丝带装饰的灰色豪华硬纸板盒。硬纸板盒更坚固，因此能更好地保护每件旗袍都不受挤压。相信该包装还能给人一种高贵典雅的感觉，并有助于促进销售，提高产品的价值。

2. 纸板盒可以印上客户定制的商标。

3. 每 10 盒装一个大纸箱，外包装用带字从外面加固，并在上面标明"远离潮湿"等字样。

Module 5　Order Confirmation

1　Learning Objectives

微课：对外贸易中的文化差异

Upon completion of this module，you should be able to：

● analyze different order letters to understand clients' different writing purposes；

● confirm an order by writing an E-mail or replying online.

2　Warm-up Questions

微课：确认订单

● Question 1：What should you do after you have received an order letter from one of your clients?

● Question 2：Is it necessary to analyze different order letters?

3　Background Knowledge

After several rounds of negotiations，a buyer will send an order lettcr to the seller informing him/her of the goods wanted. When an exporter has received such an order letter from the client, he or she should write back to confirm the order with one of the following documents attached as a simple contract to show the establishment of the deal. PO (Purchase Order), PI (Proforma Invoice) and S/C (Sales Confirmation) can all be used as simple contracts.

1. PO

A Purchase Order, or PO, is a legal document that a buyer sends to a seller to authorize a purchase. It contains the detailed information of the goods ordered by the buyer, such as commodity description, quantity, unit price, total amount, etc. A PO signed by both of the seller and the buyer can be taken as a contract.

2. PI

Many customers place orders after negotiations are completed, and will provide a formal contract or a Purchase Order to the seller. While some customers who do not have a PO to send the exporter will only require the exporter to confirm with him by a PI (Proforma Invoice) based on products, prices and delivery date, etc. Once a PI is confirmed, it is equivalent to a real contract.

A Proforma Invoice is a quotation in an invoice format made by the exporter. It can be used to apply for an import license, open a letter of credit and make a deposit. It includes the Proforma Invoice number and date, seller's name and address, buyer's name and address, detailed information of the order, the bank account of the seller, etc. After the exporter sends the PI to the importer, the latter will check it and send it back duly signed if it's correct.

3. S/C

A Sales Confirmation is issued by the seller after the buyer and the seller

新
编
外
贸
函
电

conclude a transaction through negotiation. It lists the conditions of the transaction, and is legally valid. After being signed and confirmed by the buyer and the seller, it will legally bind on both parties.

In order to write a proper order confirmation letter, we should clarify different types of order letters. Carefully analyzing the buyer's purchasing intentions will benefit both parties in business. A clearly structured order confirmation letter may diminish misunderstandings and improve communication efficiency. Generally speaking, there are three types of order letters: acceptance orders, counter-offer orders and repeat orders.

An acceptance order is an order issued directly to the seller by the buyer after receiving an offer without disagreement on the main terms of the transaction. The buyer is willing to accept the offer, and the seller only needs to deliver the goods according to the order. A counter-offer order is an order issued by the buyer when he or she has different opinions on some of the business terms offered by the seller. The counter-offer order proposes amendments to some business terms (such as packaging, shipment, method of payment, etc.), so the transaction can only be concluded after both parties reach an agreement on all the terms. A repeat order is made by a buyer who places a new order for the marketable goods again. Repeat orders normally do not change the main business terms.

4 Module-Related Correspondence

Letters Concerning Order Confirmation
➢ Letters concerning acceptance of orders
➢ Letters concerning refusal of orders
➢ Letters concerning recommending alternatives

⑤ **Sample Letters**

微课：订购信分析   微课：订购信函构成与表达

Case 1

广州蓝尔迪塑料制品有限公司外贸业务员 Leo 收到了英国客户 Cathy 发来订购太阳能泳池盖(Solar Swimming Pool Cover)的订单，根据现有库存接受订单，并及时发回订单确认函。

Letter 1：Order letter

Dear Leo，

Thank you for your quotation of March 10 and the illustrated catalogue. We find both the quality and the price satisfactory and take pleasure in enclosing our order No. 287 for solar swimming pool covers.

We note that you can supply these items from current stock and hope that they will reach us no later than Sept. 30.

Please kindly let us have your confirmation.

Yours sincerely，

Cathy

Cathy

Common Expressions

• satisfactory 令人满意的

• confirmation 确认

Useful Expressions

• illustrated catalogue 插图产品目录

• current stock 现有库存

新编外贸函电

Letter 2: Acceptance of the order

Dear Cathy,

Thank you for your letter of July 16 and the order No. 287 enclosed.

We now have pleasure in confirming that we have all the items in stock and are now making up the order. The goods can be shipped by the end of August and are due to arrive in London in September.

Enclosed is our Sales Confirmation No. 97064 made out against your order mentioned above. Please kindly countersign and return the scanned copy for our file.

It has been a pleasure doing business with you and we look forward to being of service to you again in the future.

Best regards,

Leo

Leo

Common Expressions

- Sales Confirmation 销售确认书
- countersign 会签

Useful Expressions

- have pleasure in… 很高兴……
- have all the items in stock 现货齐备
- make up the order 按订单备货
- make out against your order 依照您的订单所制
- return the scanned copy for our file 发回扫描件我方存档

Writing Tips

Structure of Acceptance of Orders

➤ Firstly, acknowledge your receipt of the order and express thanks;

➤ Secondly, inform the buyer what is underway (how and when the goods will be delivered);

➤ Thirdly, state what document has been attached to the letter for the buyer, and remind them of the payment;

➤ Finally, express good wishes for future cooperation.

Case 2

广州蓝尔迪塑料制品有限公司外贸业务员 Leo 收到了澳大利亚新客户 Mary 发来订购手摇式泳池盖收卷机(Manual Swimming Pool Cover Roller) 的订单,无法接受其发货后 30 天电汇付款的方式,致函表示不能接受,并期待对方可以做出调整以便促成交易的达成。

Letter 1: Counter-offer Order

Hi Leo,

You can find the attached order No. W235 for 300 manual swimming pool cover rollers.

We'd like to change L/C at sight into T/T 30 days after delivery.

We need the goods urgently, so please reply asap.

Sincerely,

Mary

Mary

Common Expressions

- attached 附件内的
- manual 手动的

Useful expression

- T/T 30 days after delivery 发货后 30 内电汇付款

Letter 2：Refusing an Order

Hello Mary，

Thank you for your order No. W235 for 300 manual swimming pool cover rollers.

I regret to tell you that it's our custom to do business on L/C at sight basis with new clients. We will consider T/T 30 days after delivery for the next order.

The model of pool cover roller chosen by you is very popular，and its stock is running down quickly. Considering the high quality of our goods，I am sure payment method will not hinder our cooperation.

Waiting for your favorable reply.

Best regards，

Leo

Leo

Common Expressions

- custom 习惯，常规
- hinder 阻碍

Useful Expressions

- on L/C at sight basis 在即期信用证付款的基础上

- its stock is running down quickly 库存下降很快
- payment method 支付方式
- favorable reply 肯定的回复

Writing Tips

Structure of Order Refusal

➤ Firstly，say thanks for the former order letter received from the client and express regrets for having to decline the order politely (providing some reasons will be great)；

➤ Secondly，explain why this order cannot be accepted；

➤ Lastly，express good wishes for future business.

Case 3

广州蓝尔迪塑料制品有限公司外贸业务员 Leo 收到了澳大利亚客户 Mary 发来的订单订购铝制滑道泳池盖(Aluminum Track Pool Cover)，因库存不足，致函建议对方考虑 PVC 材质的泳池盖。

Dear Mary，

We are glad to learn from your letter of 21 February that you decide to place a large order for a number of the items included in our quotation of 10 February.

All the items ordered are in stock except the 500 square meters of Aluminum Track Pool Cover. Stocks of these have been sold out after we quoted them，and it will be another four weeks before they are available again.

As you stated in your order that delivery of all items is a matter of urgency，we recommend that you consider PVC track pool covers. They are very popular with our other customers because of high quality and competitive prices. They are also operated via a remote control switch，and we offer a variety of colors for clients to choose from.

We hope you will be pleased with this suggestion.

Yours faithfully,

Leo

Leo

新编外贸函电

Common Expressions

- available 有货的
- remote control 遥控器

Useful Expressions

- all the items ordered are in stock 所有商品都有库存
- stocks of these have been sold out 库存已售罄
- they are very popular with our other customers 它们很受其他客户的欢迎

6 Field Exploring

> **Supplemental Expressions**

1. We thank you for your trial order of Aug. 18 for five hundred sets of our "Diamond" electric fans.

感谢你方 8 月 18 日订单，试订 500 台我们"钻石"牌电风扇。

新编外贸函电

Similar structures:

We {thank you for / are very much obliged for / acknowledge with thanks / are glad to receive} your order No. 1010.

We are pleased to {confirm / accept / take up} your order dated May 10.

2. You may rest assured that this order will have our careful attention.

请放心，本批订货定将妥善办理。

Similar structures:

You may be assured that this order will be {filled carefully. / executed to your satisfaction. / carried out successfully. / fulfilled in good time.}

3. We assure you that we shall effect shipment on the specified date in your order.

我们保证将按贵方订单规定的期限装运。

Similar structures:

We {assure you of our immediate action. / promise delivery next week. / guarantee to execute your order immediately. / can ensure that the work shall be done in the right way.}

4. There is a great demand for this quality, and our stock is exhausted. It will be 3 months before it is available again.

这种品质的商品需求量大，我方库存已告罄，3个月后才能再供货。

Similar structures：

> Being temporarily out of the parts you need，
>
> Since the articles you ordered are out of stock，
>
> As the goods you ordered are not in our line，
>
> Because we have not had the items for months，
>
> Due to heavy orders recently received from Japan，
>
> Because of the recent rush of orders for our goods，

we are reluctantly compelled to decline your order for the time being.

5. In view of your urgent need of the goods and the good relationship between our two parties，we have decided to accept your order in spite of the current tight supply situation，but we can do so only by putting off our supply to another customer.

鉴于你方急需此货，以及我们双方之间的友好关系，尽管目前供货紧张，我方决定接受你方订单。为此，我们不得不推迟了另一客户的交货期。

6. We hope our products will satisfy you and that you will give us the opportunity to serve you again.

希望我方产品使贵方满意，并期待今后能再次为贵方服务。

7. Our stock of M456 is exhausted，and we have no idea when the material will be restocked.

M456 号商品库存已告罄，不知何时才能补货。

8. Since your order covers such a large quantity，we are unable to meet your requirements for the moment. However，we will do our utmost to secure supply for you，and whenever the situation improves，we will not fail to let you know.

因为你方订货数量很大，我方目前不能满足你方需求。不过我方将尽最大努力为你方获取货源，一旦情况有所好转，定将及时告知。

9. As some items under your order are beyond our business scope，we can only accept your order partially. We hope this will not cause you any

inconvenience.

由于你方订单中的部分货物超出了我方的经营范围，我方只能接受你方的部分订单。希望这样不致给你方带来不便。

10. Because we are already heavily burdened with outstanding orders，it is impossible for us to accept new orders for delivery within this year.

由于我方目前已承担过多订单，因此无法接受今年之内交货的新订单。

11. Unfortunately，the recent rush of orders for our goods has made it impossible to promise shipment earlier than May 14.

不巧，由于近期我方商品订单激增，我们无法承诺在 5 月 14 日之前完成装运。

12. Unfortunately，the goods you requested cannot be supplied from stock due to heavy commitments.

很遗憾，由于订单堆积，您要的货物目前无现货可供。

13. The present supplies of raw materials are being used for earlicr orders，which makes it impossible for us to effect your shipment as required.

目前现有的原材料正用于早期的订单生产，因此我们无法按你方要求的时间交货。

14. We find it difficult to fill your order at the prices indicated in your letter because of the high cost of raw materials.

由于原材料成本高昂，我们难以按照你方来信中所示的价格供货。

15. We have to delay your order until the revised one reaches the minimum volume we have established.

只有你方把现有订货量增至我们所确定的最低数量，我们才能供货。

16. We would like to grant an accurate order by your adding the sizes on the enclosed form.

请在所附的表格中填写尺码，以确保订货准确无误。

17. The immediate shipment of your order can be expected only when you modify your usual delivery arrangements by shipping 40% in June and

新编外贸函电

the balance in July instead of two equal monthly shipments.

若你方能调整常规的交货安排，改为 6 月装运 40%，其余部分 7 月装完，而非 6、7 月各装运一半，我们才有望立刻发货。

18. Unless you place your order in March, we won't be able to deliver in

除非你方 3 月订货，否则我们无法 6 月送货。

19. The buyer is expected to make a 30% down payment.

买家需要支付 30% 货款作为定金。

20. The balance is to be paid before the delivery of the cargo.

余款需在货物交付前付清。

21. The production starts at the seller's receipt of the buyer's down payment.

订货期以收取定金作实。

22. The down payment will not be refunded if the order is cancelled by the buyer.

如买家取消订单，定金恕不退还。

23. The order will be automatically cancelled, and the down payment will not be refunded if the buyer doesn't take delivery of the cargo within 30 days beyond the due time.

如超出提货日期 30 天，订单自动取消，定金不予退回。

24. Please sign back if the above order is confirmed.

如以上订单确认无误，请签名并发回。

➢ **E-commerce Dialogue**

广州蓝尔迪塑料制品有限公司外贸员 Michael 与澳洲客户 Mr. Buick 的在线聊天记录，商议订货量及产品规格并确认 PI。

131

Buyer (Mr. Buick):

Hi, Michael. I want to see if I could get 500 m² of the foil insulation with adhesive backing. Do you have them with the parameter of 10-15 mm?

Landy (Michael):

You mean Xpe foam insulation? Let me check the parameters. Yes, we have the thicker ones like 10 mm or 15 mm.

Buyer (Mr. Buick):

What size is the roll?

Landy (Michael):

For the size, we have 1 m or 1.2 m wide, and 20 m or 25 m long.

Buyer (Mr. Buick):

I want 15 mm thick, 1 m wide and 25 m long. 15 rolls are needed.

Landy (Michael):

OK, let's confirm the specifications. Aluminum + Xpe foam + glue, 15 mm thick 1 m×25 m in size. Is it right?

Buyer (Mr. Buick):

Yes, exactly.

Landy (Michael):

Would you please provide your company name and E-mail address? I need to fill out the quotation sheet and make customer records. Thanks.

Buyer (Mr. Buick):

Sure. Our company name and E-mail address are ...

Landy (Michael):

I'm filling in the quotation sheet for you, and I will send it to you soon.

Buyer (Mr. Buick):

OK. Thanks.

Landy (Michael):

Mr. Buick, this is the quotation for you. Please have a look. If it's acceptable, I will send you the PI and payment link.

新编外贸函电

Buyer（Mr. Buick）:

Thanks. Can I make the number of 8 rolls instead of 15?

Landy（Michael）:

Sure, no problem. I will revise the PI. … Mr. Buick, please have a look at the new PI. This is the payment link.

Buyer（Mr. Buick）:

I have paid. Thanks.

Landy（Michael）:

Thank you so much. I will arrange delivery as fast as possible for you.

➤ **Foreign Trade Elite Literacy**

对外贸易中的文化意识

国际贸易已经成为世界的一种常态。了解文化如何影响世界不同地区的企业运营方式，了解哪些是不同国家可以接受的，或者为什么我们的客户行为不同，都可以对拓展业务产生影响。当我们与来自世界不同地区的客户交流时，具有文化意识是至关重要的。

那么，什么是文化意识呢？文化意识是指在与其他文化群体成员进行交流或互动时，对两种文化之间的差异和相似之处保持敏感。一个对文化敏感的人会对不同的文化、宗教、举止和沟通方式表现出开放和尊重的态度。

那么我们在对外贸易中可能会面临什么样的文化差异呢？

首先，不同国家的商务人士在信函写作上风格是不同的。例如，在日本，在称呼商业伙伴时，习惯上使用正式头衔。相反，在美国，使用名字和比较随意的口吻更常见。在德国，商务信函表达通常是直截了当和实事求是的，几乎没有闲聊的余地。相比之下，在印度，在商务信函中加入个人问候和表达祝愿是很常见的。当你给法国客户写信时，习惯上是以礼貌的问候和一些闲聊开始，然后再谈到信的主要内容。相比之下，在澳大利亚，商务信函往往更直接和切中要害。

第二，商务谈判中的不同文化。不同的文化在时间观念上不同。北美人管理时间的意识很强，他们认为时间就是金钱，所以他们在谈判中试图缩短时间；而中东和拉美人的时间观念较弱，他们更喜欢放松的日程安排和推迟回复信息。不同国家的人喜欢不同的谈判风格，谈判可以分为横向谈判和纵向谈判。横向谈判会列出所有要讨论的话题，然后同时进行讨论。纵向谈判方式是指确定所有要涵盖的问题，然后逐一讨论。

第三，来自不同文化背景的人对礼貌行为也有不同的看法。你最好留意他们对于行为方式的好恶。例如，德国人通常喜欢直接沟通。你越直截了当，沟通就越顺畅。保持严肃和避免幽默是明智之选，因为在商业环境中，笑话不受德国客户欢迎。当你邀请印度客户共进午餐或晚餐时，不要点牛肉，因为牛在印度被视为神圣的动物。

面对文化差异我们该如何应对呢？

首先，通过阅读了解不同的文化。可以阅读书籍、文章、在线资源以及与熟知不同文化的人交流。其次，到不同的国家旅行并亲身体验他们的文化也可以帮助你更好地理解文化。此外，尊重文化的差异很重要。以开放的心态对待不同的文化，并尊重他们的习俗和行为方式是很重要的。同时，也要留意别人如何理解你的文化。在你与来自不同文化的人交流时，询问他们如何理解你的文化。最后，要有耐心，花时间去理解来自不同国家的人的观点。不同文化之间的交流方式可能会有很大差异。与来自不同文化背景的人做生意比与自己相同文化背景的人做生意要花费更多的时间和精力。意识到这些差异，调整你的沟通方式，才能更好地适应对方的文化。

在国际贸易中，建立和加强跨文化意识是必要的。尽管文化意识不能保证解决所有的文化差异，但它至少为相互理解和避免冲突搭建了一个良好的开端。

⑦ Practice

❶ **Translate the Following Sentences into Chinese.**

1) Thank you for your trial order of 15 Oct. for 2,000 electric scooters.

2) We are pleased to accept your order for article No. JF100.

_____

3) We guarantee that this order will be executed to your satisfaction.

_____

4) You may be assured that this order will be fulfilled in good time.

_____

5) We promise delivery next week.

_____

6) Because we have not had the items for months, we are reluctantly compelled to decline your order for the time being.

_____

7) Due to heavy orders recently received from Japan, regretfully we are unable to accept your order at present.

_____

8) We assure you of our immediate action.

_____

9) We can ensure that the work shall be done in the right way.

_____

10) The buyer should make a 30% down payment, and the balance is to be paid before delivery.

_____

❷ **Fill in the Blanks Appropriately with the Words or Expressions Given Below.**

appreciate, promise, bear with, date, balance, in our line, satisfy, fill, take up, carry out, confirm, enter, out of stock

1) We are pleased to _____ your order No. 110.

2) You may be assured that this order will _____ successfully.

3) The goods you ordered are not _____. Please contact with other suppliers.

4) Since the articles you ordered are _____, we are reluctantly compelled to decline your order for the time being.

5) Because of recent rush of orders for our goods, we cannot _____ shipment before the end of this month.

6) It will be _____ if you can sign back the PI asap.

7) The _____ should be paid before shipment.

8) We hope our products will _____ your clients, and we may have further cooperations.

9) We _____ supply for the milling machines at the price stated in your order letter.

10) We are sorry not to be able to meet your present order request and hope that you will _____ us.

❸ **Translate the Following Letter into Chinese.**

Subject: Out of Stock

Dear Sirs,

Thank you for placing order No. 225 for 500 dozen cotton shirts with us. We regret to inform you that we are currently out of stock in the sizes you require. We do not anticipate receiving further delivery for at least another five weeks.

We apologize for any inconvenience this may cause. In the meantime, you may wish to explore other options for obtaining the shirts you need. Please rest assured that we will notify you promptly once our new stock arrives.

Thank you for your understanding.

Yours faithfully,

❹ Writing Practice.

Write a letter of acceptance of an order according to the following conditions:

已收到对方购买家具的 BD135 号订单，附上我方已签名销售确认书，请对方务必在确认书上署名并扫描发回以归档，需要对方开立信用证。告知对方收到信用证后将安排 A、B 两项货物的发货，C、D 两项货物亦将在一个月后安排船运。

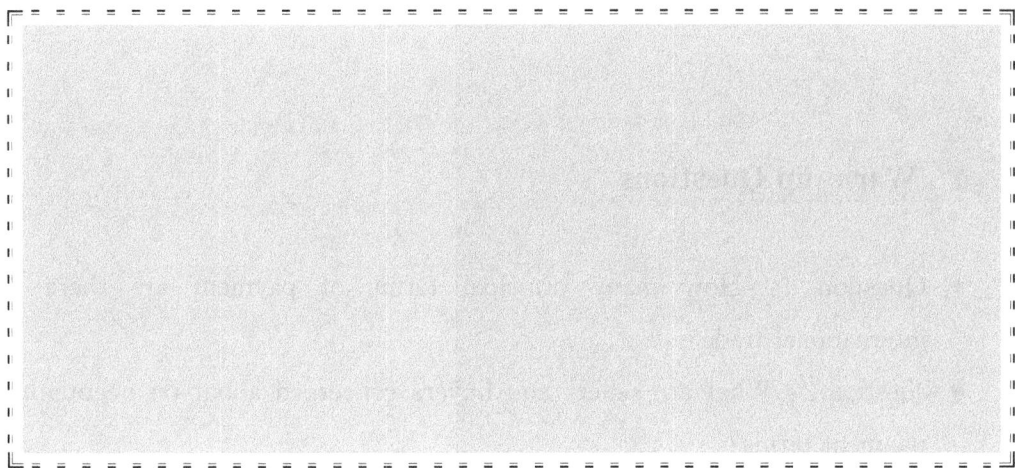

新
编
外
贸
函
电

Module 6 Terms of Payment

① Learning Objectives

微课：国际贸易结款方式

Upon completion of this module, you should be able to：

- have a basic understanding of how to negotiate the terms of payment in the clearing of international trade, namely remittance, L/C and collection, mostly focusing on L/C；
- know the structure of letters on issuing, urging and amending L / C as well as related terms and useful expressions；
- learn how to analyze cases and write letters on negotiating terms of payment in international trade.

② Warm-up Questions

- Question 1：How many principal terms of payment are there in international trade?
- Question 2：What are sellers and buyers concerned about on negotiating payment terms?
- Question 3：Which method of payment do you prefer if you are the exporter? And which one do you prefer if you are the importer?

③ Background Knowledge

The buyer and the seller find themselves inevitably confronting the money problem since they have already come into an agreement on their transaction. Typically, with domestic sales, if the buyer has good credit, sales are made on open account; if not, cash in advance is required. For export sales, these ways are not the only common methods. Many methods of payment in international trade are available, depending on how trustworthy the buyer is considered to be. None will completely eliminate the payment risks associated with international trade.

Listed in order from most secure for the exporter to the least secure, the basic methods of payment are:

- Telegraphic Transfer(T/T);
- Documentary Letter of Credit;
- Documentary Collection or Draft;
- Open account;
- Other payment mechanisms, such as consignment sales.

Among which Documentary Letters of Credit are most popularly agreed on by both the buyer and the seller since most buyers are often concerned that the goods may not be sent if payment is made in advance. Letters of credit are common in international trade because the bank acts as an uninterested party between the buyer and the seller.

Foreign trade export business adopts various payment methods, mainly including the following types:

1. Telegraphic Transfer (T/T)

微课：电汇(T/T)

Telegraph Transfer (T/T) is one of the basic ways of foreign exchange remittance business. It refers to a remittance settlement method that sends the telegram, telex or SWIFT message to the branch or agent bank in

another country indicating the remittance bank to settle a certain amount of money to the payee.

The method of Telegraph Transfer is characterized by simple operation, and the payee can receive the remittance quickly. The risk is relatively low for the buyers, so it is adopted by most companies.

Common telecommunication methods are: SWIFT, telex (TELEX), telegraph (CABLE, TELEGRAM), etc.

Telegraph Transfer is divided into T/T in advance or deposit (advance payment) and T/T after shipment (payment after shipment or after receipt).

T/T in advance or deposit means that after the contract is signed, the buyer shall pay a part of the deposit (usually 30%). The seller will then complete the production, notify the buyer of payment, and receive the balance before delivering the goods.

T/T after shipment means that the balance will be paid after the shipment. The seller will arrange the production and shipment after receiving the deposit, the customer will pay the balance after receiving the copy of the document, and the seller will send a full set of documents after receiving the balance.

At present, Telegraphic Transfer is a widely used remittance method, and its business process is as follows: the application form of Telegraphic Transfer from the remittor and payment to the remitting bank first, and then the remitting bank sends the remittance information to the receiving bank via a confidential telegram or telex, and sends a transfer notification to the recipient. The payee receives payment and debit notifications from the bank, including payment, settlement, and remittance bank information. At the same time, the bank transfers the transfer information to the payer as a receipt.

Compared to a Letter of Credit in transactions, but the fee paid to the bank is much lower than that of a Letter of Credit.

新编外贸函电

The process of T/T payment method

（一）电汇（Telegraphic Transfer, T/T）

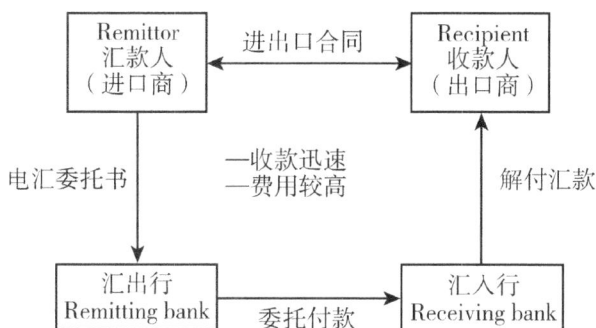

2. Letter of Credit（L/C）

A letter of credit is a written guarantee document issued by the bank（the issuing bank）according to the requirements and instructions of the buyer（the applicant）with a certain amount of payment according to the specified documents of the buyer（the beneficiary）.

微课：信用证概述

A letter of credit is a kind of bank credit where the bank bears the first payment responsibility. It is a relatively safe way for the seller.

Operation Process of Documentary Credit

1. The buyer and seller stipulate in the trade contract that payment shall be made using a documentary letter of credit.

微课：跟单信用证
操作流程

2. The buyer shall notify the local bank（issuing bank）to open a letter of credit in favor of the seller.

3. The issuing bank requests another bank to notify or confirm the letter of credit.

4. The notifying bank notifies the seller that the letter of credit has been opened.

5. After receiving the letter of credit and ensuring that it can fulfill the conditions stipulated in the letter of credit，the seller shall ship the goods.

6. The seller shall submit the documents to the designated bank. The bank may be the issuing bank or the payment，acceptance，or negotiation

bank specified in the letter of credit.

7. The bank reviews the documents according to the letter of credit. If the documents comply with the provisions of the letter of credit, the bank will make payment, acceptance, or negotiation in accordance with the provisions of the letter of credit.

8. Banks other than the issuing bank shall send the documents to the issuing bank.

9. After the issuing bank verifies that the documents are correct, it shall repay the bank that has already made payment, accepted or negotiated under the letter of credit in a agreed form.

10. The issuing bank shall present the documents to the buyer after payment, and then the buyer shall collect the goods against the documents.

How does paying with a letter of credit work?

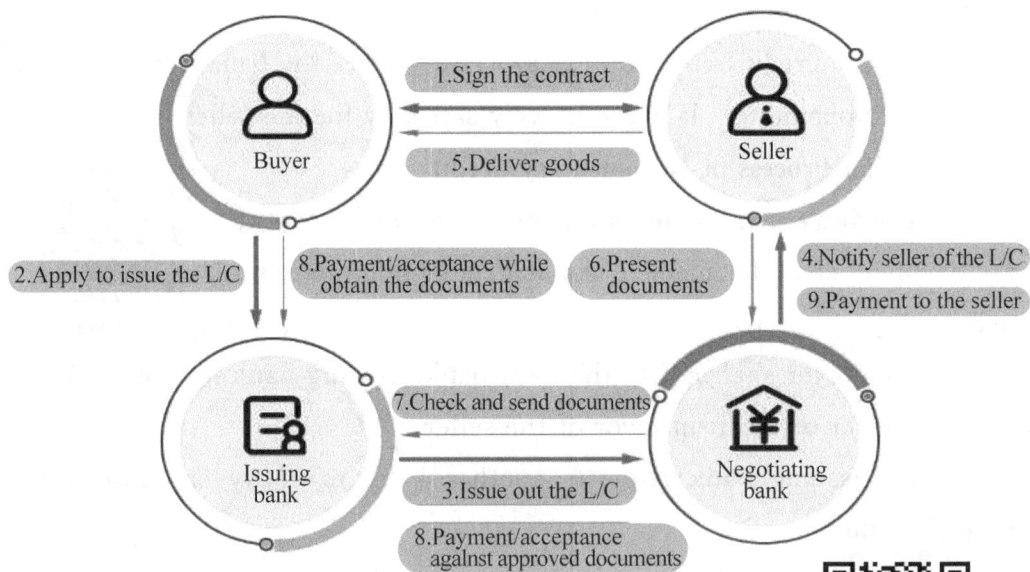

• **Types of L/C**

Letters of credit may be classified into the following types:

微课：信用证的种类

• documentary L/C/clean L/C 跟单信用证/光票信用证

- revocable L/C/irrevocable L/C 可撤销信用证/不可撤销信用证
- confirmed L/C/unconfirmed L/C 保兑信用证/不保兑信用证
- sight payment L/C/ usance L/C 即期信用证/远期信用证
- transferable L/C /untransferable L/C 可转让信用证/不可转让信用证
- divisible L/C/undivisible L/C 可分割信用证/不可分割信用证
- revolving L/C 循环信用证
- L/C with T/T reimbursement clause 带电汇条款信用证
- back to back L/C/reciprocal L/C 对背信用证/对开信用证

Elements of a Letter of Credit

Applicant：The person who applies to the bank to issue an L/C，i. e. the importer or actual buyer.

微课：信用证的开立

Opening bank；issuing bank：Accepts the commission of the issuing party，opens an L/C，and assumes the responsibility of ensuring payment. Usually this is the bank in the location of the importer.

Advising bank：Entrusted by the issuing bank to transfer the L/C to the exporter's bank. Only proves the authenticity of the L/C and assumes no other obligations. It is usually the bank in the exporter's location and is usually the agent bank of the issuing bank.

Beneficiary：The person designated on the L/C as having the right to use the certificate，namely the exporter or actual beneficiary.

Documents Concerning L/C Required

The letter of credit is a distinct and separate transaction from the contract on which it is based. All parties deal in documents and not in goods. Payment under a documentary letter of credit is based on documents，not on the terms of sale or the physical condition of the goods. Typically，the documents called for under an L/C will include：

Financial Documents

- Bill of Exchange

- Co-accepted Draft

Commercial Documents

- Invoice
- Packing List

Shipping Documents

- Transport Document
- Insurance Certificate
- Commercial，Official or Legal Documents（as required）

Official Documents

- License
- Embassy legalization
- Origin Certificate
- Inspection Cert
- Phyto-sanitary Certificate

Transport Documents

- Bill of Lading（ocean or multi-modal or Charter party）
- Airway bill
- Lorry/truck receipt
- railway receipt
- CMC other than Mate Receipt
- Forwarder Cargo Receipt，etc.

（if there are other specific types not listed）

Insurance Documents

Insurance policy，or Certificate but not a cover note.

However，the list and form of documents are open to imagination，and negotiation and might contain requirements to present documents issued by a neutral third party evidencing the quality of the goods shipped or their place of origin.

3. Collection

D/P and D/A are both type of documentary collections, and there are two delivery methods for documentary collections: D/P for payment and D/A for acceptance.

微课：付款交单(DP)
承兑交单(DA)

Document against Payment (D/P)

D/P (Document against Payment) is a method of settlement by which the collecting bank can deliver the commercial documents to the importer only after the importer has paid up.

D/P payment documents are mainly divided into two types: sight documents and forward documents.

D/P at sight refers to the situation where the exporter issues a sight draft which is then submitted to the importer by the collecting bank. The importer must pay by sight draft. After the payment is made, the importer will receive the shipping documents, and the payment will be delivered together with the documents representing the ownership of the goods.

Documents against Acceptance (D/A)

D/A (Documents against Acceptance) is also a commonly used payment method in international trade. The exporter instructs the collecting bank, through the corresponding bank channels to release ownership and other shipping documents to the importer after the importer accepts the bill of exchange.

D/A, requires the buyer to obtain the shipping documents before making payment, in order to take delivery of the goods. This means the importer gets hold of shipping documents and takes delivery of the goods before payment. So the exporter would have to take great risks. Therefore, exporters maintain a strict control attitude towards adopting this method.

新
编
外
贸
函
电

④ Module-Related Correspondence

Upon reading the procedures for operating a L/C, we find that the buyer, the seller, and the banker have to keep in touch with each other so that the transaction would be executed in a sound manner. There are usually several kinds of letters concerning L/C which may travel through between the buyer and seller, or the banker.

- The letter concerning negotiating the terms of payment;
- The letter concerning urging the establishment of L/C;
- The letter concerning amending the L/C.

⑤ Case Study

微课：商榷付款方式信函

- **Negotiating the terms of payment**

In foreign trade correspondence, negotiating the payment terms between the seller and the buyer is a crucial step, as it directly affects the smooth progress of the transaction and the protection of both parties' interests.

Some steps and key points to consider when negotiating payment terms include:

- Understanding common payment methods and their characteristics;
- Analyzing the specific situation of the transaction.

Nature and amount of goods:

Different goods and amounts may require different payment methods. For example, large-amount transactions may be more suitable for relatively secure payment methods such as letters of credit.

Trading partners and background:

Different countries and regions have different trading habits and preferences, requiring the selection of appropriate payment methods based on specific situations.

Trade terms and contract clauses：

Trade terms and contract clauses are important bases for choosing payment methods，and they need to be consistent with the contract.

Proposing reasonable payment suggestions：

Based on understanding the specific situation of the transaction，the seller can propose reasonable payment suggestions. For example，if the transaction amount is large and both parties have good creditworthiness，a letter of credit may be suggested; if the transaction amount is small and the buyer has good creditworthiness，collection may be suggested. When proposing payment suggestions，the advantages of the method and possible fees involved can be explained in detail to help the buyer better understand and accept them.

Writing Structure

The letter discussing the method of payment is divided into three parts：

➢ Indicate which letter you are responding to and state that you cannot accept the other party's method of payment；

➢ State the reason why you require your specific payment method；

➢ Be confident and urge acceptance of payment terms；

➢ State that you hope the other party will accept your proposal.

Sample Letters

Case 1

广州蓝尔迪塑料制品有限公司外贸业务员小陈收到了中东客户的订购游泳池盖（Swimming Pool Cover）的订单，与客户签订的合同中已明确了付款方式是保兑的、不可撤销的、可分割的、循环的、可转让的、以我方为抬头人的信用证。但是客户订单中的付款方式是 50％使用见票 30 天信用证，其余 50％采用见票付款交单。小陈礼貌地拒绝他们的付款方式，并给出了拒绝的理由。

新编外贸函电

Dear Sirs,

Thank you for your order No. 908 for 100 square meters of Swimming Pool Cover, but we regret being unable to accept your terms of payment, 50% by L / C at 30 days' sight, the balance 50% by D / P at sight.

The specimen contract we sent you last time indicates clearly that our usual terms of payment are by confirmed, irrevocable, divisible, revolving and transferable letter of credit in our favor, available by draft at sight, reaching us at least 30 days ahead of shipment and remaining valid for negotiation at our counter till the 15th day after the final date of bill of lading, and permitting transshipment and partial shipments. We also mentioned in our letter on 20 July that several big British firms had already done business with us on the above terms basis. We hope you would agree with us on payment terms so as to get the initial transaction through.

As soon as we get your confirmation, we will airmail you the contract for counter signature.

We are looking forward to your favorable reply.

Yours faithfully,

Jack Chen

Jack Chen

Common Expressions

- order No. 订单号
- terms of payment 付款条件
- L/C Letter of Credit 信用证
- at sight 即期
- D/P Document against Payment 付款交单
- D/A Document against Acceptance 承兑交单

- divisible 可分割的

- revolving 循环的

- transferable 可转让的

- negotiation 议付

- in one's favor… 以……为受益人

- initial transaction 首次交易

- counter signature 会签

Useful Expressions

- regret being unable to accept your terms of payment 很遗憾不能接受您的付款条件

- our usual terms of payment are … 我们通常的付款条件是……

- in our favor 以我们为受益人

- available by draft at sight 凭即期汇票支付

- reaching us at least 30 days ahead of shipment 在装运前至少 30 天到达我处

- remaining valid for negotiation at our counter till the 15th day after the final date of bill of lading 并在提单最后日期后的第 15 天内在我们柜台保持有效

- permitting transshipment and partial shipments 允许转运和部分装运

- get the initial transaction through 完成首笔交易

- airmail you the contract for counter signature 通过航空邮件向您发送合同以供双方签字

- looking forward to your favorable reply 期待您的积极回复

Case 2

广州蓝尔迪塑料制品有限公司外贸业务员小陈收到了另一澳洲客户的来信，由于各种原因，客户希望小陈公司同意修改付款方式。下面是小陈收到的客户来信。

新编外贸函电

Dear Sirs,

We enclose our order No. 463. We have examined the specifications and price list for your range of Swimming Pool Cover and now wish to place an order with you.

As we are in urgent need of new stock, we would be grateful if you would make up the order and ship it as soon as possible.

In the past we have traded with you on a sight credit basis. We would now like to propose a different arrangement. When the goods are ready for shipment and the freight space booked, you notify us and we then remit the full amount by telegraphic transfer (T/T).

We are asking for this concession so that we can give our customers a specific delivery date and also save the expense of opening a letter of credit. We believe that as this arrangement should make little difference to you, but should help our sales; so we trust that you will agree to our request.

We look forward to receiving confirmation of our order and your agreement to the new arrangements for payment.

Yours faithfully,

Tony

Tony

Sales Manager

Common Expressions

- specifications 规格
- price list 价格表

- range 系列

- stock 库存

- shipment 发货

- freight space 货运空间

- notify 通知

- remit 汇款

- telegraphic transfer（T/T）电汇

- concession 让步

- delivery date 交货日期

- confirmation 确认

Useful Expressions

- place an order with you 向你方下订单

- be in urgent need of 急需

- trade with you on a sight credit basis 以即期信用证方式与你方交易

- propose a different arrangement 提出不同的安排

- notify us and we then remit the full amount by telegraphic transfer（T/T）
通知我们后，我们将通过电汇方式支付全额款项

- give our customers a specific delivery date 给我们的客户提供具体的交
货日期

- save the expense of 节省……的费用

- should make little difference to you 对你方来说影响不大

- help our sales 有助于我们的销售

- confirmation of our order 我们订单的确认

- agreement to the new arrangements for payment 对新支付安排的协议

- feel free to contact us 随时与我们联系

Case 3
广州蓝尔迪塑料制品有限公司外贸业务员小陈收到要求修改付款方式

的函电，他认为对方理由合适，跟经理汇报后，回复了客户，同意修改付款方式。

Dear Tony，

Thank you for your letter of 10 July. We are pleased to receive your order No. 123 of the same date for our black tea.

We are pleased to accept the modified payment terms. A fax has been dispatched to you about this. All the items in your order can be supplied from stock and packed and shipped immediately your remittance by telegraphic transfer is received.

We will airmail you the following documents immediately after shipment

1. Bill of lading in duplicate；
2. Invoice，CIF London，in triplicate；
3. Insurance policy for 110% of invoice value；
4. Guarantee of quality.

We will，of course，notify you as soon as your order is shipped.

Yours sincerely，

Xiao Chen

Xiao Chen

Export Manager

Common Expressions

● payment terms 支付条款

● Telegraphic Transfer 电汇

● Bill of Lading 提单

● invoice 发票

- CIF（Cost，Insurance，and Freight）成本加保险费加运费
- Insurance Policy 保险单
- guarantee of quality 质量保证书
- shipment 发货
- airmail 航空邮件

Useful Expressions

- We are pleased to … 我们很高兴……
- A fax has been dispatched to you about this. 我们已经就此向您发送了传真。
- Your remittance by telegraphic transfer is received. 已收到您的电汇汇款。
- All the items in your order can be supplied from stock. 您的订单中的所有商品都有现货。
- Packed and shipped immediately 立即进行包装和发货
- Immediately after shipment… 发货后立即……
- In duplicate/triplicate 一式两份/一式三份
- For 110% of invoice value 发票价值的 110%
- Notify you as soon as 一旦……就通知您
- Your order is shipped 您的订单已发货

Writing Tips

➤ **Communicate and Negotiate with the Buyers**

After proposing payment suggestions，it is necessary to fully communicate and negotiate with the buyer. This can be done through foreign trade correspondence，telephone，video conferences，or other means to discuss and negotiate issues such as payment methods，payment time，and payment amount in detail. During the communication and negotiation process，it is important to maintain patience and politeness，respect the opinions and needs of the other party，and actively seek solutions acceptable by both parties.

> **Reach an Agreement and Sign the Contract**

After sufficient communication and negotiation, if both parties reach an agreement on payment terms and other issues, a formal foreign trade contract can be signed. The contract should clearly stipulate the payment method, payment time, payment amount, and other relevant clauses to ensure the smooth progress of the transaction and the protection of both parties' interests.

In summary, negotiating payment terms in foreign trade correspondence requires careful consideration and sufficient communication. By understanding common payment methods and their characteristics, analyzing the specific situation of the transaction, proposing reasonable payment suggestions, communicating and negotiating with the buyer, and reaching an agreement and signing a contract, we can ensure the smooth progress of the transaction and the protection of both parties' interests.

- **Urging Establishment of L/C**

In the export contract, if the buyer and the seller agree to pay by letter of credit, the buyer shall open a letter of credit on time in strict accordance with the provisions of the contract.

微课：催开信用证

If the contract does not specify the time for the buyer to issue the letter of credit, the buyer should issue it within a reasonable time, as timely issuance by the buyer is a prerequisite for the seller's normal performance.

But in practical business, sometimes foreign importers often delay the issuance of letters of credit, or intentionally do not open letters of credit when there are changes in the market or shortages of funds. In this regard, we should urge the other party to quickly handle the procedures for opening the letter of credit. Especially for bulk commodity transactions or specially designed commodity transactions at the request of buyers, timely reminders should be made based on stock availability.

Urging the Opening of a Letter of Credit is Beneficial

➤ The significance of urging the opening of a Letter of Credit is that it allows the exporter to perform the contract smoothly.

➤ The significance of urging the opening of a Letter of Credit is for the exporter to conduct transactions based on the basis of shipment and document preparation.

The mastery, management, and use of Letter of Credit during the performance of contracts for payment under Letter of Credit are directly related to the safety of foreign exchange collection and the important work related to the performance of contracts by import and export enterprises.

A Letter of Credit is related to the shipment, presentation of documents, and final payment of goods. The exporter will only arrange shipment upon receipt of the Letter of Credit issued by the importer, otherwise the goods will not be shipped and delivered in a timely manner.

➤ Therefore, when the export enterprise has not received the letter of credit, exporter should urge the importer to open the Letter of Credit as soon as possible to ensure that the transaction can be carried out according to the contract.

➤ In practical business, the most commonly used method for foreign trade personnel to urge the issuance of Letters of Credit is to send E-mails, which are referred to as "push letters".

Writing Tips

The letter urging the establishment of L/C is divided into four parts:

➤ Mention the relevant contract or order.

➤ Reference the contract number and date; Point out the urgency of the shipment or delivery date. State that the Letter of Credit (L/C) has not been received yet.

➤ Request for Action Paragraph: Urge the recipient to expedite the issuance of the L/C. Remind the recipient to ensure that the L/C stipulations are in line with the contract terms.

> Closing Paragraph：Express the expectation of receiving the L/C promptly. Emphasize the importance of the shipment or delivery deadline. Politely end the letter.

Sample Letters

Case 1

广州蓝尔迪塑料制品有限公司与中东的客户签订的那批货已经备妥了，但是到现在为止，还没有收到买家的信用证。一定要收到对方的信用证并核对无误后，公司才能发货。于是小陈写了一封催证函给他们，请他们尽快开立信用证，以保证及时履行合同。

Dear Sirs，

With regard to your order No. 123 for 100 square meters of Swimming Pool Cover，we regret that up to this date we have received neither the required credit nor any further information from you.

Please note that，as agreed，the terms of payment for the above board rare–sight Letter of Credit should be established within 2 weeks upon the arrival of our sales confirmation.

We hereby request you to open by cable an irrevocable sight Letter of Credit for the amount of in our favor，with which we can execute the above order according to the original schedule.

We are looking forward to your favorable reply.

Yours faithfully，

Xiao Chen

Xiao Chen

Sales Manager

新编外贸函电

Common Expressions

- irrevocable 不可撤销的

- sight 即期（指信用证需即期付款）

- amount 金额

- sales confirmation 销售确认书

- expedite 加快

Useful Expressions

- Regarding your order No. 123 关于您的订单编号 123

- We regret that … 我们很遗憾……

- As agreed, … 按照协议，……

- We hereby request you to … 我们特此要求您……

- Open by cable an irrevocable sight Letter of Credit 通过电报开立不可撤销即期信用证

- In our favor 以我方为受益人

- Execute the order 执行订单

- According to the original schedule 按照原计划

- We are looking forward to your favorable reply. 我们期待您的积极回复。

Case 2

The letter in Which the Seller Urges the Establishment of L/C

Dear Mr. Brian,

With reference to the goods under our Sales Confirmation No. 3456, we wish to draw your attention to the fact that the date of delivery is approaching, but we have not yet received the covering L/C to date. Please do your utmost to expedite the same, so that we may execute the order smoothly. In order to avoid subsequent delay, please see to it that the L/C stipulations are in exact accordance with the terms in the Confirmation.

We hope to hear favorably from you soon.

Yours truly,

Xiao Chen

Xiao Chen

Common Expressions

- with reference to 关于
- the date of delivery 交货日期
- approaching 即将发生的
- covering 相关的
- do one's utmost 尽最大努力
- execute the order 完成订单，执行订单
- stipulation 条款

Useful Expressions

- With regards to … 关于……
- We are concerned to note that … 我们关切地注意到……
- It is of utmost importance to us that … 对我们来说，……是极其重要的
- Kindly ensure that … 请确保……
- In strict compliance with … 严格符合……
- To prevent any further delays, … 为了防止任何进一步的延误，……
- We look forward to … 我们期待……
- We remain hopeful for a favorable response from you. 我们仍然希望您能给予一个满意的答复。

新编外贸函电

Case 3

The Letter in Which the Seller Urges the Establishment of L/C

Dear Mr. Brian，

Sales Confirmation No. 3456

We refer to our E-mail dated 8th June and our fax of June 12th，urging you to open the L/C covering the captioned Sales Confirmation，and we regret to say that up to the present we haven't received any news from you.

We have to remind you that we did agree before we placed the order that you would establish the required L/C upon receipt of our Sales Confirmation. Needless to say，we are placed in a very embarrassing situation，now that two months have passed and nothing whatsoever has been done by you. As the goods have been already for shipment for quite some time，it behooves you to take immediate action，particularly since we cannot think of any valid reason for further delaying the establishment of the said credit.

Yours truly，

Xiao Chen

Xiao Chen

Common Expressions

- Sales Confirmation 销售确认书
- behoove 应该，必须(在此处为古英语用法，表示"有必要")
- embarrassing 尴尬的
- delay 延迟
- Credit 信用(在此处指信用证)

Useful Expressions

● We refer to our E-mail dated … and our fax of … urging you to … 我们参考了日期为……的电子邮件和日期为……的传真，催促您……

● We regret to say that up to the present we haven't received any news from you. 我们遗憾地说，到目前为止我们还没有收到您的任何消息。

● We have to remind you that … 我们必须提醒您……

● We did agree before … that you would … 我们在……之前已经同意您会……

● Needless to say, we are placed in a very embarrassing situation … 不用说，我们现在处于一个非常尴尬的境地……

● As … have been … for quite some time, it behooves you to … 由于……已经……有一段时间了，您必须……

● We cannot think of any valid reason for further delaying … 我们想不到任何合理的理由来进一步延迟……

● Please take immediate action to ensure the smooth progress of our transaction. 请立即采取行动以确保我们交易的顺利进行。

● If you have any questions or require further information, please do not hesitate to contact us. 如果您有任何疑问或需要进一步的信息，请随时与我们联系。

Case 4

The Letter in Which the Buyer Notifies the Seller the Establishment of L/C

Dear Sirs,

We have received your letter asking us to establish a Letter of Credit for the Sales Confirmation No. 102. This is due entirely to negligence in work of our staff. This morning we have opened an L/C with our banker of BOC Changsha.

Please ship the goods in time and send us shipping advice after loading the goods on board of the vessel.

Best regards.

Sincerely yours,

Xiao Chen

Xiao Chen

Common Expressions

- negligence 疏忽

- open 开立

- banker 银行家(在此处指银行)

- Bank of China（BOC）中国银行

- goods 货物

- Shipping Advice 装船通知

- vessel 船舶

- voyage 航次

- estimated arrival date 预计到达日期

- partnership 合作伙伴关系

Useful Expressions

- due to negligence in work 由于工作上的疏忽

- open an L/C with 在……银行开立信用证

- ship the goods in time 及时装运货物

- send shipping advice 发送装船通知

- Look forward to continuing our business relationship. 期待继续我们的业务关系。

- Please do not hesitate to contact us. 请随时与我们联系。

161

新编外贸函电

Writing Tips

Here Are Some Tips for Writing a Letter Urging the Issuance of a Letter of Credit.

➤ **Maintain politeness yet assertiveness:** In the letter, you need to express your request in a polite tone while also firmly communicating your expectation of receiving the Letter of Credit as soon as possible.

➤ **Clearly list key information:** In the letter, clearly state the contract number, transaction goods, transaction amount, delivery deadline, and other key information to help the recipient quickly understand the context.

➤ **Specify the L/C requirements:** List in detail your specific requirements for the letter of credit, including the type, amount, validity period, payment terms, etc. , to ensure there are no omissions or ambiguities.

➤ **Provide necessary supporting documents:** If possible, attach any supporting documents related to the application for the Letter of Credit, such as a copy of the contract, order confirmation, shipping schedule, etc. , to help the recipient better understand your needs.

➤ **Emphasize the time sensitivity:** If the delivery deadline is approaching, be sure to emphasize this in the letter to remind the recipient of the urgency and the need for prompt action.

➤ **Use formal and professional language:** Maintain a formal and professional tone in your writing, avoiding overly casual or informal expressions.

➤ **Check spelling and grammar:** Before sending the letter, carefully check for any spelling or grammar errors to ensure the professionalism and readability of the correspondence.

➤ **Include contact information:** At the end of the letter, clearly provide your contact information so that the recipient can easily reach out to you if needed.

➤ **Follow up:** After sending the letter, if you do not receive a response within a reasonable time, it is advisable to follow up to confirm whether the recipient has received your request and to inquire about the progress.

➤ **Comply with international trade rules and practices:** When writing the request for the Letter of Credit, ensure that you comply with international trade rules and practices to ensure that your request meets relevant standards and requirements.

● **L/C Amendment**

After the L/C has been opened, the seller should examine the L/C very carefully. As a foreign trade salesman, we should have careful, rigorous working attitude and good professional quality. As for checking and examining the L/C, it means that the stipulations in L/C should be in conformity with those in contract. If the seller finds some discrepancies, they have to inform the buyer to make some amendments. It is very important to review the L/C carefully, to see whether there are any discrepancies. A small carelessness can bring a huge loss to the company.

微课：撰写改证函

The Process of Amending the L/C:

➤ The beneficiary first examines the L/C based on the contract.

➤ If the beneficiary find something wrong, that is, the terms of L/C don't agree with those of contract, the seller will notify the buyer by E-mail.

➤ Then the beneficiary will make an application through the opening bank to make an amendment.

➤ After that, the opening bank will advise the advising bank.

● **Discrepancies Commonly Found Between the L/C and Supporting Documents**

➤ Letter of Credit has expired prior to presentation of draft.

➤ Bill of Lading evidences delivery prior to or after the date range stated in the credit.

➤ Stale dated documents.

➤ Changes included in the invoice not authorized in the credit.

> Inconsistent description of goods.

> Insurance document errors.

> Invoice amount not equal to draft amount.

> Ports of loading and destination not as specified in the credit.

> Description of merchandise is not as stated in credit.

> A document required by the credit is not presented.

> Documents are inconsistent as to general information such as volume, quality, etc.

> Names of documents not exact as described in the credit.

> Beneficiary's information must be exact.

> Invoice or statement is not signed as stipulated in the letter of credit.

When a discrepancy is detected by the negotiating bank, a correction to the document may be allowed if it can be done quickly while remaining in the control of the bank. If time is not a factor, the exporter should request that the negotiating bank return the documents for corrections.

If there is not enough time to make corrections, the exporter should request that the negotiating bank send the documents to the issuing bank on an approval basis or notify the issuing bank by wire, outline the discrepancies, and request authority to pay. Payment cannot be made until all parties have agreed to jointly waive the discrepancy.

Writing Tips

> At the beginning of the letter, clearly point out that the received letter of credit (L/C) is inconsistent with our contract or sales confirmation.

> List clearly the specific terms and conditions of the L/C that require modification, as well as the changes that need to amend. For instance, the shipment date, insurance amount, and commission percentage.

> Kindly request that the buyer respond to the seller's request by

promptly amending the L/C according to seller's requirements and sending us a new copy of the amended L/C.

➤ Look forward to prompt response and cooperation.

Sample Letters

Case 1

广州蓝尔迪塑料制品有限公司小陈收到了客户开来的信用证，但是他发现信用证与合同有几处不相符合的地方。经过认真审核，小陈找出了不符合的地方，并且马上给客户回复了邮件，请客户修改信用证。

Dear Sirs，

We have received with thanks your L/C No. 6678 established against S/C No. 20230506，but much to our regret，there are some discrepancies between the L/C and the S/C. Hereby we list them as follows for your attention.

1. According to S/C No. 20230506，your L/C shall allow "TRANSSHIPMENT" instead of "TRANSSHIPMENT PROHIBITED".

2. "Shipment is to be made in a single lot not later than August 26，2023" should be amended to "shipment should be effected in two equal lots within August".

3. The port of shipment is "Guangzhou" instead of "Shanghai".

We would like you to make the necessary amendments immediately. As you know, we will be unable to make shipment unless the above discrepancies are corrected. Looking forward to your early amendments for the relevant L / C.

Best regards，

Xiao Chen

Xiao Chen

Common Expressions

- L/C (Letter of Credit) 信用证
- S/C (Sales Contract) 销售合同
- discrepancy 不符
- transshipment 转运
- amendment 修正
- port of Shipment 装运港

Useful Expressions

- We have received with thanks your L/C No. … established against S/C No. …

我们已收到贵方针对……号销售合同的……号信用证并表示感谢。

- much to our regret，there are some discrepancies between the L/C and the S/C.

遗憾的是，信用证与销售合同之间存在一些不符之处。

- According to S/C No…. , your L/C shall allow … instead of " … "

根据……号销售合同，贵方信用证应允许……，而不是"……"。

- Shipment is to be made … should be amended to " … "

装运应在……，应修改为"……"。

- The port of shipment is … instead of …

装运港是……，而不是……。

- We would like you to make the necessary amendments immediately.

请您立即做出必要的修正。

- As you know，we will be unable to make shipment unless the above discrepancies are corrected.

如您所知，除非上述不符之处得到修正，否则我们将无法进行装运。

- Looking forward to your early amendments for the relevant L/C.

期待贵方尽快对相关信用证进行修正。

Case 2

The Letter in Which the Seller Requests the Seller to Amend the L/C

Dear Sirs,

Your L/C No. 2345

Covering 100 square meters of Swimming Pool Cover

The above L/C stipulates direct shipment and allows no transshipment. It would be quite in order, were it not for the fact that direct steamers are at present few and far between. The only near opportunity is the s. s. "Flying Cloud", on which, unfortunately, it is impossible to book any tonnage on account of congestion of cargoes.

Under the circumstances, we find it necessary to request you to amend your L/C as allowing transshipment, and failing that the delivery of this order will be forced to be delayed beyond the contractual date.

We are cabling you today to the above effect and shall appreciate it if you will telegraph the modification as requested.

Yours truly,

Xiao Chen

Xiao Chen

Common Expressions

- dozen 打（一种数量单位，常用于纺织品）
- direct Shipment 直接装运
- transshipment 转运
- steamers 轮船

- congestion of cargoes 货物拥挤
- Telegraph（Telegraphy）电报
- modification 修改

Useful Expressions

- The above L/C stipulates … 上述信用证规定……

- It would be quite in order，were it not for the fact that … 如果不是因为……，它将会很合适

- We find it necessary to request you to … 我们发现有必要请求你 ……

- Failing that … 如果未能……

- The delivery of this order will be forced to be delayed beyond the contractual date. 这批订单的交货将被迫延迟到合同日期之后。

- We are cabling you today to the above effect. 我们今天正就此事向贵方发电报。

- Shall appreciate it if you will … 如果贵方能……，我们将不胜感激

- Amend your L/C as allowing transshipment 修改贵方信用证以允许转运

Case 3

The Letter in Which the Buyer Requests the Seller to Amend the L/C

Dear Sirs，

Your L/C No. 4567

100 square meters of Swimming Pool Cover

We thank you for your L/C No. 4567 for 100 square meters of Swimming Pool Cover. We are sorry that owing to some delay on the part of our manufacturers，we are unable to get the goods ready before the end of this month. We sent you a fax yesterday asking you to extend the shipment to May 15th and validity to May 30th.

新编外贸函电

It is expected that the consignment will be ready for shipment in the early part of May and we are arranging to ship it on s. s. "Nellore" sailing from Shanghai on 10 May.

We are looking forward to receiving your extension of the above L/C, thus enabling us to effect shipment of the goods in question.

Yours faithfully,

Xiao Chen

Xiao Chen

Common Expressions

- metric ton 公吨
- delay 延迟
- shipment 装运
- validity 有效期
- consignment 货物
- effect shipment 安排装运
- sailing date 起航日期

Useful Expressions

- We are sorry that owing to some delay on the part of our manufacturers, we are unable to get the goods ready before the end of this month.

我们很抱歉由于制造商的延迟，我们无法在本月底之前准备好货物。

- We sent you a fax yesterday asking you to extend the shipment to May 15th and validity to May 30th.

我们昨天给您发了一份传真，请求您将装运期延长至 5 月 15 日，并将信用证有效期延长至 5 月 30 日。

● It is expected that the consignment will be ready for shipment in the early part of May and we are arranging to ship it on s. s. "Nellore" sailing from Shanghai on 10 May.

预计该货物将在 5 月初准备好装运，我们安排于 5 月 10 日从上海起航的"Nellore"号货轮装运。

● We are looking forward to receiving your extension of the above L/C, thus enabling us to effect shipment of the goods in question.

我们期待收到您对上述信用证的展期，从而使我们能够安排相关货物的装运。

Writing Tips

Here Are the Steps to Follow:

➢ Precisely determine the specific details that require rectification.

➢ Select an appropriate format and style in accordance with the standards of your industry or organization. Maintain a formal yet cordial tone.

➢ Utilize a clear and specific heading at the commencement of the letter, such as "Regarding [Specific Matter]".

➢ Furnish the accurate information or documentation, and enclose the revised documents or detailed specifications.

➢ Ensure the letter is concise and to the point, avoiding unnecessary verbosity and intricate sentences.

(5) **Field Exploring**

Supplementing Useful Sentences

1. To cover our shipment, we request you to establish a commercial letter of credit in our favor for the contracted amount through a Japanese bank.

我们要求贵方通过一家日本银行开立以我方为受益人的相当于合同金额的商业信用证。

Similar structures:

As agreed,	the terms of payment are by irrevocable L/C, payable by sight draft.
	payment is to be made against sight draft under L/C.
	we only require 100% value, confirmed and irrevocable L/C payable at sight.
	our business terms are L/C sight draft.
	we insist that payment be made against L/C instead of D/A.
	we cannot accept Cash against documents on arrival of goods at destination.

2. In as much as the amount involved is rather small, we agree to draw on you by your documentary draft at sight on collection basis, but this should not be regarded as a precedent.

由于涉及金额较小，我们同意按托收办法向贵方开具即期跟单汇票，但只此一次，下不为例。

Similar structures：

With a view to further developing trade dealings between us

As a special sign of encouragement，

As an exception，

In consideration of the very pleasant business relationship we've had with you，

In order to develop friendship with you in the wake of expansion of business，

For good order's sake，

we are agreeable to D/P payment.

3. As arranged，we are handing you our bill of exchange for US $ 120,000 and ask you to protect it upon presentation.

根据约定，我们现随函给你们开具 120,000 美元即期汇票一张，请见票即付。

Similar structures：

Please surrender these Documents to the drawee against their accepting

the draft and

collect and remit the net proceeds to us.

give the draft their protection.

give our draft their due honor.

ask them to duly meet our draft.

tell them to confirm if this is acceptable to them.

4. Your draft of 30th June has been accepted and will be given our protection.

贵方 6 月 30 日汇票已承兑，到期照付。

Similar structures：

In settlement of the amount of your invoice，we

enclose a check for
enclose a bank draft for
have instructed our bank to remit
have transferred
agree to let you credit our No. 5
account with

US $ 145,000 which pays your account

in full.

5. We are sorry that we could not ship the goods by a May vessel only because of the delay of your L/C. Please open the said L/C at once.

我们感到遗憾，由于贵方信用证耽误，我们的货不能装 5 月份的船。请速速开立上述信用证。

Similar structures：

We regret that up to now we haven't received your L/C yet；please

attend to this matter with all speed.
do your utmost to ensure the payment without delay.
arrange for the credit immediately.
expedite the said L/C very soon.
rush a credit without any further delay.
take up this matter with the issuing bank at once.
push the confirming house for their soonest action.

6. Your L/C has been received this date，but we would request you to amend it as follows.

贵方信用证今日收到，但请按下述意见修改。

173

Similar structures：

You are kindly requested to	amend the said L/C as follows. have the L/C amended to read "2% more or less". make necessary amendment for the L/C at an early date. have the relative credit include "Transshipment Not Allowed". increase the amount of your L/C by US＄380. 000. rush the amendment to the L/C.

7. This has made us impossible to ship the goods within the lifetime of L/C that expires on May 10.

我们不可能在信用证 5 月 10 日到期交货。

Similar structures：

Under the circumstances，we earnestly hope that you will

extend arrange for a three-week extension of instruct your bankers for the extension of validity of allow us a further extension of give us ample time to negotiate the draft under ship the goods to us before the expiration of effect shipment within the validity of	the L/C to the end of

this month.

Under the circumstances，we earnestly hope that you will have your L/C extended before it expires.

8. Enclosed we hand you a statement of account to date，showing a balance of US＄45,000 in our favor，which we trust will be found in order.

随函寄去财务报告一份，请查收。至今贵公司尚欠我方美金 45,000 元。

Similar structures：

Be good enough to favor us with your check for US＄54,000

long overdue.

due on our statement for October.

in our favor.

in settlement of our account rendered.

still owing on our statement of 30th March.

the unpaid balance on your account.

that will clear off the outstanding balance.

that pays your account in full.

9. The financial difficulties from which we are suffering at present are the cause of our inability of meeting your draft at maturity.

我公司目前财务困难，在贵方汇票到期时无力付款。

Similar structures：

In this case，I regret very much to say that

I find myself unable to meet this bill due on August 10th.

we shall be unable to meet this draft.

we have accordingly declined to accept your bill.

we have told our accounting not to process payment.

our draft on you dated 18th July was returned dishonored by our bank.

you have overcharged me by an amount of US＄3,000.

we will be delaying payment.

10．We opened an L/C in your favor through the Citi Bank this morning.

今早，我们经由花旗银行开立了一个以你方为受益人的信用证。

11. Today we have opened an irrevocable L/C in your favor for the amount of US＄9,000 covering our order No. 3422 with the Bank of China, Dalian.

我们今天通过中国人民银行大连分行就第 3422 号订单开立了以你方为受益人的不可撤销的信用证，金额为 9,000 美元。

12. For payment we require 100％ value，irrevocable L/C in our favor with partial shipment allowed clause available by draft at sight.

我们要求用不可撤销的、允许分批装运、金额为全部货款、并以我方为抬头人的信用证，凭即期汇票支付.

13. To do so，you could save bank charges for opening an L/C.

这样做，你们可以省去开证费用。

14. It's expensive to open an L/C because we need to put a deposit in the bank.

开证得交押金，因此花费较大。

15. We pay too much for such a letter of credit arrangement.

这种信用证付款方式让我们花费太大了。

16. There will be bank charges in connection with the credit.

开立信用证还要缴纳银行手续费。

17. A letter of credit would increase the cost of my import.

信用证会增加我们进口货物的成本。

18. The seller will request to amend the letter of credit.

卖方要修改信用证。

19. Your refusal to amend the L/C is equivalent to cancellation of the order.

你们拒绝修改信用证就等于取消订单。

20. The port of shipment is Shanghai instead of Guangzhou.

装运港是上海，不是广州。

➢ **E-commerce Dialogue**

广州蓝尔迪塑料制品有限公司外贸员 Walter 与澳洲客户 Mr. Rick 的对话，询问支付选项的基本细节和客户的偏好。

Landy（Walter）：

Hello，Mr. Rick！We have your order ready. We offer credit card，PayPal，or bank transfer as payment options. Which one would you like to use？

Buyer（Mr. Rick）：

Hi there！PayPal sounds good to me. It's easy and secure.

Landy（Walter）：

Perfect！I'll send you a PayPal invoice right away. Once it's paid，we'll ship your order out.

Buyer（Mr. Rick）：

Great，thank you. I'll look out for the invoice and make the payment soon.

Landy（Walter）：

You're welcome！If you have any questions or need help with the payment，just let me know. Have a nice day！

Buyer（Mr. Rick）：

Thanks again. Have a good day！

● 催促尽快付款

Landy（Walter）：

Hi！About your order ♯12345，it's still waiting for payment.

Buyer（Mr. Rick）：

Oh yeah，sorry about that. I forgot.

Landy（Walter）：

No worries. Could you pay soon? It'll help us ship faster.

Buyer（Mr. Rick）：

Sure，doing it now.

Landy（Walter）：

Awesome，thanks! We'll ship it out soon and let you know.

Buyer（Mr. Rick）：

Cool，thanks. Bye!

➢ **Foreign Trade Elite Literacy**

结款的沟通技巧

在与外商沟通付款事宜时，具备以下素养是至关重要的，这些素养不仅有助于确保沟通的顺畅，还能促进双方的合作与信任。

一、专业知识与技能

了解国际支付方式：熟悉各种国际支付方式，如电汇（T/T）、信用证（L/C）、付款交单（D/P）、承兑交单（D/A）等，以及它们的操作流程、风险点和费用结构。这有助于在沟通中提供准确的信息和建议。

掌握汇率知识：了解汇率的波动规律及其对付款金额的影响，能够在沟通中为客户提供有关汇率风险的建议和解决方案。

熟悉国际贸易法律法规：了解国际贸易相关的法律法规，特别是与付款相关的条款和规定，以确保沟通内容的合法性和合规性。

二、沟通与协商能力

清晰表达：能够用准确、简洁的语言表达付款要求、条件和期限，避免产生误解和歧义。

耐心倾听：认真倾听外商的意见和需求，理解其关切和疑虑，以便更好地进行沟通和协商。

灵活应变：在沟通中遇到问题时，能够灵活应对，提出多种解决方案，以达成共识和协议。

维护关系：保持友好、专业的态度，尊重对方的文化和习惯，以维护双方的良好合作关系。

三、风险意识与防控能力

风险评估：对付款过程中可能遇到的风险进行识别和评估，如信用风险、汇率风险等，并制定相应的防控措施。

合同管理：确保合同条款清晰、完整、具有法律约束力，特别是在付款条件、违约责任等方面要有明确的约定。

监控与跟进：在付款过程中保持对款项流向和进度的监控和跟进，确保款项按时、足额到账。

四、诚信与责任感

诚实守信：在沟通中保持诚实守信的原则，不夸大其词、不隐瞒真相，以赢得外商的信任和尊重。

责任心强：对付款事宜负有高度的责任心，确保每一个环节都按照约定和计划进行，不出现疏漏和差错。

五、跨文化交流能力

了解文化背景：了解外商所在国家和地区的文化背景、商业习惯和礼仪规范，以避免在沟通中出现文化冲突和误解。

尊重文化差异：在沟通中尊重外商的文化差异和个性特点，采用适当的沟通方式和语言风格，以建立和谐的沟通氛围。

⑦ Practice

❶ **Translate the Following into English.**

1. 汇票

2. 保兑行

3. 出票人

4．议付

5．欠款

6．转船

7．催款单

8．托收

9．提单

10．分批装运

❷ Translate the Following into Chinese.

11．in question

12．Expedite

13．cash against documents

14．Protect

15．few and far between

16．for this end

17．at maturity

18．Dishonor

19．Render

20．surrender

❸ Fill in the Blanks with Appropriate Words According to the Hints Given.

1．We hope that you will ac _____ us in this respect，as before，and continue giving us li _____ discounts on your basket ware.

2．To square the account of the charges on this order，we are sending you herewith a draft for the con _____ sum through the Bank of Montreal，who has been instructed to hand over do _____ against payment of the draft.

3. We hope you will understand when we explain that the urgency of your order left with insufficient time to make the usual inquiries about the terms of payment and that we therefore had no choice but to follow our standard p _____ with new customers of placing the tr _____ on a ca _____ basis.

4. Since the shipment falls d _____ next week, we kindly request you to have the said credit ex _____ accordingly.

5. In fact, we are perfectly willing to dispatch your orders by means of co _____, p _____ that the total value in _____ does not exceed $ 4,000 for one contract.

6. We wish to draw your attention to the fact that the date of delivery is ap _____, but we still have not received your c _____ Letter of Credit up to now.

7. In order to avoid subsequent a _____, kindly see to it that the L/C st _____ are in exact accordance with the terms of the Contract.

8. As our draft has been returned pr _____, we kindly request you to adjust the matter with your bankers and give it your pro _____.

9. Because the relative credit has failed to reach us to d _____, we insist that you ex _____ same without any further delay.

❹ **Fill in the Following Blanks with Proper Prepositions and Then Translate the Sentences into Chinese.**

1. When the shipment is made, you may value _____ us _____ the invoice amount, _____ three month's date, agreeably _____ your terms, and at the same time advise us _____ it by E-mail.

_____

_____

2. Please be good enough to favor us _____ your check, _____

US$ 9,000 _____ settlement of our account rendered _____ 31st May.

_____

_____

3. We regret to remind you that we have not received payment of the balance of HK $ 5,000 due _____ our statement _____ December, sent to you on 2nd January.

_____

_____

4. We were much surprised, _____ referring _____ our books, to note that your account amounting _____ £46,000 long overdue, remains unpaid _____ the last letter we have sent you regarding it.

_____

_____

5. Having made repeated applications _____ payment of this amount _____ avail, we now give you notice that we shall take _____ a summons _____ recovery of the same.

_____

_____

6. Our Mr. Smith is _____ in Honolulu _____ an urgent business, and will not return until the 21th July, so if you will kindly let the matter stand over _____ then, we shall credit our account _____ the residue French Francs 4,000 _____ our outstanding balance.

_____

_____

7. Please give us one more month _____ the completion of the goods and instruct your bankers _____ the extension of validity _____ ample time for us to negotiate the draft _____ this credit.

_____

_____

8. We would request you to take _____ this matter with the issuing bank at once and let us know what has become _____ the letter of credit otherwise, contrary _____ our intention, the shipment may be delayed a great deal.

_____

_____

⑤ **Translate the Following Sentences into English.**

1. 为了进一步发展我们之间的贸易，我方同意付款交单。

_____

_____

2. 我方非常遗憾的是至今尚未收到你方信用证；请尽快办理此事。

_____

_____

3. 我方随函附上 112,000 美元银行汇票一张以全额结清你方发票账目。

_____

_____

4. 请开立一个 20 公吨苹果的信用证，金额为 2 万美元。

_____

_____

5. 今天，我方收到由美国花旗银行开出的以你方为付款人的金额为 3,500 美元的信用证。

_____

_____

6. 请按下述意见修改第 205 号信用证。

_____

_____

7. 兹附寄第 50 号信用证的修改通知。

_____

_____

8. 不允许分批装运应改为允许分批装运。

_____

_____

9. 装运港是上海，不是大连。

_____

_____

10. 开证行应是中国银行而不是花旗银行。

_____

_____

⑥ **Please Write a Letter for Amending the L/C Based on thc Following Writing Situation.**

写作情景：

1) 广州迅捷家电进出口有限公司（Guangzhou Xujie Home Appliance Import & Export Co，Ltd）于 2019 年 6 月 1 日收到泰国 HM 公司（Thai HM Corporation）开来的张不可撤销的即期信用证 No.123456.

2) 我方收到信用证后，立即对该证进行审核，发现信用证存在几处与合同不相符的地方。

3) 由于进口方开证晚，导致我方装船延误，需要延展装船日期和信言用证的有效期。

4) 我公司销售经理 Lug 致函泰国 HM 公司采购部经理 Jim，要求对方修改并延展该信用证。

经审核，需要修改的不符点如下：

1) 货物数量"450 台"应女为"500 合"。

2)汇票的付款期限"见票后 30 天付款"应改为"见票即付"

3)装运港"秦皇岛"应改为"大连"。

4)最迟装运日和信用证的有效期应分别延展至 2019 年 7 月 10 日和 2019 年 7 月 31 日。

新编外贸函电

Module 7　Shipment

微课：国际贸易货运方式

① Learning Objectives

Upon completion of this module，you should be able to：

- be able to contact the seller to urge shipment and advise the buyer of the shipment；
- get familiar with the writing plans，useful phrases and sentences for effecting shipment.

② Warm-up Questions

- Question 1：How do people transport the goods in international trade？
- Question 2：What should the seller and the buyer agree on for sea transport？
- Question 3：What is the main work included in the shipment？
- Question 4：How many parties are involved in the shipment？

③ Background Knowledge

Shipment is one of the essential links in the chain of international trade. It signifies the seller's fulfillment of the obligation to make delivery of the goods.

1. Choice of Carriage Methods

The choice of carriage methods depends on the nature of the products, the distance to be shipped, available means of transportation, and relative freight costs. Generally speaking, goods can be transported by road, rail, air, parcel post, but in most cases of international trade, about 98% of world trades are covered by sea transport. Sea transport has many advantages, such as easy passage, large capacity and low cost.

The modern way of sea transportation in international trade is that the cargo is transported by container ships. A shipping container is a container with strength suitable to withstand shipment, storage, and handling. Containers are constructed of metal and are of standard lengths ranging from 10 to 40 feet. There are also temperature-controlled containers specially provided for the types of goods that need them. The advantages of container service are obvious. Containers can be loaded at factory premises or at nearby container bases, and mechanical handling enables cargoes to be loaded in a matter of hours rather than days, which reducing the time ships spend in port and greatly increasing the number of sailings.

2. Terms of Shipment

The terms of shipment are the requirements of shipment agreed by both the exporter and the importer who enter into the sales contract.

In a sales contract, a sales confirmation or a Letter of Credit, terms of shipment are indispensable. Usually, terms of shipment are as follows:

1) Modes of transport;

2) Time of shipment;

3) Port of loading and unloading;

4) Shipping advice;

5) Partial shipment and transshipment;

6) Shipping documents, etc.

3. Main Work Included in the Shipment

In international trade, effecting shipment to the buyer is one of the seller's major obligations under the sales contract. Getting the goods transported to the destination is a very complicated process and covers rather a wide range of work. In practice, shipment involves such procedures such as:

1) clearing the goods through the customs;

2) booking shipping space or chartering a ship;

3) completing shipping documents;

4) dispatching shipping advice, etc.

4. Parties Involved in Shipment

As the time of shipment is stipulated in the contract, it requires the seller to fulfil the obligation quickly, carefully and economically, and to avoid business risks reasonably. There are three parties involved in the movement of goods:

1) the consignor or the shipper (who sends goods);

2) the carrier (who carries the goods);

3) the consignee (who receives the goods at the destination);

4) These three parties should stay in frequent contact and letters concerning shipment are frequently used.

5. Shipping Documents

Shipping documents are forms that accompany a shipment listing the date shipped, the customer, the method of shipment, and the quantities and specifications of goods shipped.

Shipping documents are prepared by the exporter or the freight forwarder. They allow the shipment to pass through customs, to be loaded onto a carrier, and be transported to the destination.

新编外贸函电

Key shipping documents include：

1）commercial invoice 商业发票

2）packing list 装箱单

3）certificate of origin 原产地证明

4）certificate of insurance 保险单

5）bill of lading 提单

4 Module-Related Correspondence

Although the buyer and the seller have agreed on the shipping terms in the contract，they still need to communicate by letters or E-mails on matters related to the shipment before the goods arrive at the destination port. For example，informing the establishment of L/C and instructing the packing and shipping marks，informing the goods ordered are ready for dispatch，name of the vessel，date of departure and estimated time of arrival，etc.

Letters Concerning Shipment：

➢ Letters concerning shipping instructions

➢ Letters concerning urging shipment

➢ Letters concerning shipping advice

5 Case Study

微课：装运指示信函

● **Shipping Instructions**

Before shipment，the buyers generally send their shipping requirements to the sellers，informing the packing，shipping mark，mode of transportation，etc. ，known as the shipping instructions.

Case 1

一个美国客户在广州蓝尔迪塑料制品有限公司订购一批游泳池贴膜（PVC Swimming Pool Liner），现致函蓝尔迪公司的外贸跟单员小林，告知已开具订单相关的信用证，并做出装运指示，告知其所订船期、包装和唛头要求。

Dear Mr. Lin,

With reference to our order No. 332 for 200 rolls PVC Swimming Pool Liner（聚氯乙烯泳池贴膜），we are glad to inform you that a letter of credit in your favor has been opened yesterday. We have booked shipping space on SS MINGZHU sailing from Nansha Port to Liverpool on 30th July. Please get the goods ready for shipment at an early date and do your utmost to ship them by that vessel without delay.

We would like to remind you that the goods should be packed each in one polybag and outer-packed in a cardboard with reinforced bottom，10 cartons to one carton measuring 5×3×3 feet and weighing about 100 pounds. Meanwhile，please see to it that the shipping marks indicated in our order and the gross net weights are to be stenciled on each case.

We trust the above instructions are clear to you and the shipment will give our users' entire satisfaction.

Sincerely yours,

Wilson Smith

Wilson Smith

Common Expressions

- with reference to 关于……
- book shipping space 订舱

- get the goods ready for shipment 备货待运

- do your utmost 尽一切努力

- without delay 不延误

- reinforced bottom 加固底托

- measure 体积为……

- weigh 重量为……

- stencil 刷（唛头）

- give … entire satisfaction 令……完全满意

Case 2

一家外国公司致函广州的一家灯具外贸公司，告知相关信用证已开具，请求将订单中的水晶灯装指定船只发出。

Gentlemen，

In reply to your letter dated 19，we are pleased to advise that the confirmed，irrevocable Letter of Credit No. 1132 for the amount of USD15,000 was established through the Commercial Bank，New York on July 8. Upon receipt of the same，please deliver our order No. 668 for crystal chandeliers per s. s. "Elizabeth" with ETA on August 16，2024 at Boston. We also ask you to see to it that all the goods are well packed，so as to avoid damage in transit.

We shall appreciate your close co-operation in this respect and await your shipping advice by fax.

Yours faithfully，

Common Expressions

- 表示"发货"：

1）make delivery of goods

2）make/effect shipment

3) deliver/ship/dispatch the goods

● in reply to … 兹复……

● Commercial Bank 商业银行

● upon receipt of … 一旦收到

● crystal chandeliers 水晶吊灯

● with ETA on … 预计抵达时间为

1)-ETD (estimated time of departure) 预计出发时间

2)-ETA (estimated time of arrival) 预计到达时间

● see to it that … 请注意

● so as to 以便

● appreciate your close co-operation 感谢您的密切合作

● in this respect 在这方面

Useful Expressions

Here are some sentence patterns we use to give shipping instructions.

1. Please ship the first lot under Contract No. 552 by s. s. "Chinese Rose" scheduled to sail on or about August 9.

请于 8 月 9 日左右将第 552 号合同项下的第一批货由中国玫瑰号轮运出。

Similar structures:

Please ship the subject goods	by the first available steamer.
	before November 25, 2024.
	not later than July 31, 2024.
	between October/ November, 2024.
	from November 2023 to February 2024.

2. Since the purchase is made on FOB terms, you are to ship the goods from Hong Kong on a steamer to be designated by us.

由于该交易是按 FOB 条款成交的，你方应从香港将货装上我方指定的轮船。

3. Our customer requests the shipment is to be made in three equal lots，each every two months.

我们的客户要求将货物分成三批等量装运，每两个月装一批。

Similar structures：

The goods are to be shipped in three monthly lots of 20 tons each on separate bills of lading.

货物分 3 个月装运，每批 20 吨，提单分开。

Writing Tips

●**Structure of Shipping Instruction**：

➤ Part 1：Informing the opening of L/C，with necessary information such as opening date，bank，total amount，L/C number，etc.

➤ Part 2：Informing the ETD and ETA，mode of transportation，name of vessel，etc.

➤ Part 3：Informing the packing，shipping mark，etc. and asking for punctual delivery.

●**Urging Shipment**：

A letter urging shipment can be used in two ways：

微课：催促装运信函

➤ When the buyer is in urgent need of the lot，he may write to the seller and ask for an earlier shipment.

➤ Another situation is that the date of shipment is approaching rapidly，but the buyer has not received the shipping advice concerning the lot. A letter of this kind is written to require punctual shipment within the contracted time.

Case 1

法国 ABB 进口商从广州蓝尔迪塑料制品有限公司订购了 2 000 个泳池灯（Swimming Pool Lights），现在发货日期快到了，蓝尔迪公司的业务员小林收到了一封买方来信，敦促在规定时间内按时发货。

Urging Immediate Shipment

Dear Mr. Lin,

Our order No. FNQ-652

Referring to the captioned order for 2,000 Swimming Pool Lights, we wish to draw your attention to the fact that up to the moment, we have not received any information from you concerning this shipment.

When we placed this order we explicitly pointed out that punctual shipment was of special importance because our customers were in urgent need of the goods and we had given them a definite assurance of early delivery.

Under the circumstances, it is obviously impossible for us to extend L/C No. 558 again, which expires on 16th October. We hope you will make every effort to effect shipment within the stipulated time as any delay would cause us much trouble and financial loss.

Sincerely yours,

Wilson Smith

Wilson Smith

Common Expressions

● referring to 关于

● captioned 标题所示的

● draw your attention to the fact that 请你注意

e. g. We wish to draw your attention to the fact that the goods are to be transshipped at Hong Kong.

我们想提请你方注意，货物将在香港转船。

- concerning 相关的

e. g. This E-mail is concerning the insurance of the goods under L/C WT855.

这个邮件是关于 WT855 号信用证项下货物的保险事宜。

- explicitly 明确地

- be of special importance 非常重要的

e. g. Making sure that the stipulations of L/C are in accordance with the terms of sales contract is of special importance.

确保信用证条款与合同条款一致是至关重要的。

- in urgent need of … 急需

e. g. We are in urgent need of this shipment because the sales season is approaching.

由于销售旺季来临，我们急需此货。

- given sb. a definite assurance of 向……保证

e. g. The buyer gives us a definite assurance of opening L/C within 2 weeks.

- under the circumstances 在这种情况下

e. g. Under the circumstances，we suggest you accept the alternatives to catch the sales season.

在这种情况下，我们建议你们接受替代品，以赶上销售旺季的需求。

- make every effort to：*do your utmost to* 尽你所能

e. g. Please make every effort to ship the steel in two equal lots，each 1,000 tons.

请尽量把这批货按两批发送，每批 1 000 吨。

- effect shipment 发货

e. g. Effecting shipment timely is one of the seller's obligations.

- stipulated time （合同/信用证）规定的时间

Case 2: Asking for Earlier Shipment

因气温骤降，羽绒服库存告急，一家外国公司致函深圳的一家外贸公司，恳请提前发货。

Dear Mr. Wilson,

According to contract No. 256 covering 2,600 down coats（羽绒服），the shipment is to be made in November. But yesterday our customers informed us that they need this consignment urgently to fulfill the orders with their buyers，as the weather suddenly turned very cold last week and the down coats enjoyed good sale in our market. For this reason，we find ourselves under the necessity of requesting your cooperation to advance shipment to October.

We can imagine the inconvenience which our request may cause you，but we do hope our old pleasant relations will offset them.

Thank you for your cooperation in this respect. Your favorable replay will be highly appreciated.

Sincerely yours，

Common Expressions

- according to 根据
- urgently 紧急地、迫切地
- fulfill the orders 执行订单
- find ourselves under the necessity of 有必要
- advance to 提前到
- cause inconvenience 带来不便

Case 3：Urging Punctual Shipment

英国某公司向广州某公司订购了一批货物，现致函该公司，告知相关信用证已开具，并建议了合适的发货时间和运输船只，以敦促出口方按时发货。

Dear Sirs，

Re：Your Sales Confirmation No. 568 Covering 1600 Panda TV Sets

We thank you for your letter dated 15th November in connection with the captioned goods. In reply，we take pleasure in advising you that the confirmed，irrevocable Letter of Credit No. 489 for the sum of USD 480,000, has been opened this morning through the Royal Bank of Canada.

Upon receipt of the same，please effect shipment of the goods booked by us as soon as possible. We are informed by the local shipping company that s/s "Milk Way" is due to sail from Shenzhen to our port on or about the 20th November and，if possible，please try your best to ship by that steamer.

Should this trial order prove satisfactory to our customers，we can assure you that repeat orders in increased quantities will be placed. Your close co-operation in this respect will be highly appreciated. In the meantime，we await your shipping advice by fax.

Yours faithfully，

Common Expressions

- in connection with 与……相关的
- in reply 兹复
- take pleasure in 很高兴……

新编外贸函电

- on or about 大约在……（时间）
- repeat orders 重复订单
- close co-operation 密切合作
- be highly appreciated （受到）高度赞赏
- in the meantime 同时

Useful Expressions

Here Are Some Sentence Patterns That We May Use to Urge Shipment.

1．To Remind the Exporter of When to Ship the Goods or to Mention the Non-Receipt of Shipping Notice.

1）We regret to remind you that the contractual shipment date has passed，but no advice has been received from you concerning the execution of our order for 200 metric tons of rice.

我们很遗憾地提醒你方，合同规定的装运期已经过去了，但关于我方订购的 200 吨大米的装运情况，你方仍未提供任何信息。

2）According to the terms of Contract No. 318，shipment is to be effected by the 20th Jan.，and we must have the B/L by the 31st at the latest.

按照 318 号合同条款，货物应于 1 月 20 日前装运。我们最迟需在 1 月 31 日前拿到提单。

3）We refer to Contract No. AP457 signed between us on August 1，2022 for digital cameras，which stipulates that the latest shipment date is October 15，2022.

我们于 2022 年 8 月 1 日签订的 AP457 号关于数码相机的合同规定，最迟装船期为 2022 年 10 月 15 日。

4）We are eager to know the details about the shipment of the 10 containers of bathroom equipment we ordered last month.

我们迫切想知道上月我们所订的 10 个集装箱浴室设备的具体发运情况。

2. To State the Reason Why Punctual Shipment is Required

1）As our company is in urgent need of the goods，we would like to emphasize again the importance of the punctual shipment within the validity of the L/C.

因为本公司急需这批货物，所以我们想再次强调在信用证有效期内准时装运的重要性。

2）Please strictly adhere to the latest shipment date indicated in the L/C because our distributors have been waiting for the arrival of these Chinese art crafts with high anticipation.

请严格遵照信用证中有关最迟装运期的规定，因为我们的分销商们一直在满怀希望地等待着这批中国工艺品的到达。

3）Delay of the shipment will lead to irretrievable disastrous loss when the Christmas season passes.

延误装运期会带来不可挽回的巨大损失，因为到时圣诞节的销售旺季已过。

3. To Urge Timely or Earlier Shipment and Indicate the Consequences of the Exporter's Action of Shipment

1）We request you to make serious efforts to get the ordered goods dispatched within the prescribed time limit.

请务必认真努力，以期在规定的期限内发货。

2）As the goods have not yet been dispatched，we must ask you to ship them without any further delay. If the order is not executed within the stipulated time，we shall have to cancel it.

由于货物未运出，我们必须要求你方尽快发货，不得再有任何延误。如你方未能在规定时间内执行订单，我们将取消订货。

Similar structures：

We	have to impress on you the need for urgent shipment
	trust that you will make all necessary arrangements to ship the goods
	rely on you to execute this order
	have to ask for your assurance that the shipment will be made
	must insist on your delivery
	are completed to lay emphasis upon your dispatch
	must have the B/L from you

within the prescribed time limit.

3）We would ask you to cooperate with us in advancing the shipment to the end of September to enable us to catch the brisk demand in Christmas sales season.

请你方予以配合，将装运期提前至 9 月底，以便我们能够赶上圣诞销售旺季。

4）In case you should fail to effect the shipment by the end of this month，we would have to lodge a claim against you for the loss as is stipulated in the sales confirmation signed by both of us in January of this year.

如果贵方才能在本月底前完成发货，我们将不得不根据今年 1 月双方签署的销售确认书中的有关规定，向贵方提出索赔。

5）If your first consignment is promptly delivered and proves to conform to the samples，we confirm that we are quite willing to place more orders.

如果贵方的首批货物能及时交付，且产品品质与样品相符，我们确认后将非常乐意下更多的订单。

Writing Tips

Structure of Letters to Urge Shipment：

➢ Part 1：identify the relative order or contract and mention the no-receipt of shipping advice.

➢ Part 2：emphasize the importance of punctual shipment.

➢ Part 3：stress the validity of L/C and urge the seller to ship the goods immediately.

• Asking for earlier shipment：the shipping date required here is earlier than the agreed date. A letter of this kind is written when the buyer is in urgent need of the goods and wants it to reach you at an earlier date.

• Urging immediate shipment：when there has been a delay in punctual shipment，the buyer may urge an immediate delivery，or it may lead to the cancelation of contract.

• Asking for punctual shipment：after the opening of L/C，the buyer may write a letter of this kind to ensure shipment at stipulated date and thus to avoid delay.

• **Shipment Advice**（装船通知）

After making shipment，the seller should promptly advise the buyer of its effectuation，no matter whether the transaction is concluded on FOB，CFR or CIF basis. For FOB and CFR transactions，the buyer will have to effect insurance on the shipment upon receipt of shipping advice from the exporter. Moreover，the importer may know when to receive the goods and arrange with a customs broker for the cargo clearance.

微课：装运通知信函

Requirement of shipping advice is agreed by both parties and can usually be found in terms of L/C：

1）SHIPMENT ADVICE WITH FULL DETAILS INCLUDING SHIPPING MARKS, CTN NUMBERS, VESSEL'S NAME, B/L NUMBER，VALUE AND QUANTITY OF GOODS MUST BE SENT ON THE DATE OF SHIPMENT TO US. 装运通知应列明包括运输标志、箱号、船名、提单号、货物金额和数量在内的详细情况，并在货物发运当天寄开证行。

2）BENEFICIARY MUST FAX ADVICE TO THE APPLICANT FOR THE PARTICULARS BEFORE SHIPMENT EFFECTED AND A COPY

OF THE ADVICE SHOULD BE PRESENTED FOR NEGOTIATION. 受益人需在货物装运前传真发出装运通知，传真副本作为议付单据提交。

3) SHIPMENT ADVICE QUOTING THE NAME OF THE CARRYING VESSEL，DATE OF SHIPMENT，NUMBER OF PACKAGES，SHIPPING MARKS，AMOUNT，LETTER OF CREDIT NUMBER，POLICY NUMBER MUST BE SENT TO APPLICANT BY FAX，COPIES OF TRANSMITTED SHIPMENT ADVICE ACCOMPANIED BY FAX TRANSMISSION REPORT MUST ACCOMPANY THE DOCUMENTS. 表明船名、装船日期、包装号、唛头、金额、信用证号、保险单号的装船通知必须由受益人传真给开证人，装船通知和传真副本以及发送传真的电讯报告必须随附议付单据提交。

Case 1

广州某数码产品贸易公司的业务员小肖收到新加坡进口商已开具信用证的通知后，安排将订单货物发出，并致函对方，告知发货时间、船名、预计到达时间等信息，并随函附上相关单证。

Dear Miss Fang，

Thank you for your L/C dated December 3rd，2007.

We are now writing to confirm our fax dispatched just now informing you that your P/C No. 201ZCBE3012 dated Dec，3rd for 2,000 pcs No. P1001 Mobile called "Panda P95" has been shipped today from Guangzhou by vessel May Flower，which is due to arrive at your port on about January 20th.

Enclosed please find copies of following documents：

2 Non-negotiable B/L；

1 Commercial Invoice No. 0932；

1 Insurance Policy；

1 Inspection Certificate；

新编外贸函电

We have drawn a draft at sight for the invoice amount under the French Bank, Paris L/C No. 2525 through China Bank, Guangzhou to whom all documents have been handed.

We shall be pleased to hear in due course that the consignment has arrived safely and in good order.

Yours Sincerely,

Reta Xiao

Reta Xiao

Sales Manager

Common Expressions

- dispatched 发货

- via 经由（运输工具）

- due to 预计

e. g. This consignment of goods is due to arrive at your port by the end of this week.

这批货预计本周末抵达你港。

- Enclosed please find … 随函附上

- documents 单据

- Non-negotiable B/L 不可转让提单

- Commercial Invoice 商业发票

- Insurance Policy 保单

- Inspection Certificate 查验单

- in due course：*eventually，at the appropriate time* 在适当的时候

e. g. The arrangements will be published in due course.

计划将在适当的时候公布。

● consignment：*the goods delivered* 这批货物

e. g. The first consignment of food has already left the port.

运送的第一批食品已经离开了港口。

● in good order：*in good condition* 状态良好的

e. g. It seems to me that everything here is in good order.

我觉得这里一切正常。

Case 2

出口商广州蓝尔迪塑料制品有限公司的外贸业务员小林刚刚收到法国 ABB 公司的来信，敦促他们交货。现在货物已经准备好发货了。小林需要写一封信告知买家装运消息。

Dear Mr. Smith，

Your Order No. FNQ-652

We write to inform you that we have today shipped the 2,000 Swimming Pool Lights by M. S. "Flying Cloud" sailing tomorrow, September 29th, from Guangzhou. We trust the goods will reach you safely and give you every satisfaction.

As desired, we have drawn upon you for the invoice amount $60,000 at three month's date. Herewith, we hand you the invoice and the bill of lading, both of which we trust you will find in order.

All items were individually examined before being packed and we trust they will reach you safely. We should be glad if you would unpack and examine them as soon as possible after deliver, and in the event of any breakage, notify us at once.

Yours sincerely，

Lin

Lin

Common Expressions

- give you every satisfaction 令你方满意

- as desired 如您所愿

- drawn upon you 向你方开票

- individually 分别地、单独地

- unpack 开包、开箱

- in the event of 如遇……

- breakage 破碎、破损

Useful Expressions

Here Are Some Sentence Patterns That We May Use to Advice Shipment.

1. To Inform the Importer of Details of the Shipment

1）We are pleased to advise that your order No CM556 covering 4,000 dozen shirts dated July 5th under L/C No. 9326 has been shipped via S/S "Princesses", which is estimated to depart from Guangzhou on Sep. 15th and estimated to arrive at Newport on Oct. 15th.

我们很高兴地通知贵方，您 7 月 5 日订购的 4 000 打衬衣（订单编号 CM556，信用证编号 9326）已装"公主"轮，预计 9 月 15 日从广州出发，预计 10 月 15 日抵达新港。

2）We write to inform you that we have today shipped the 500 antique potteries and 300 porcelain wares by M. S. "Flying Cloud", which is sailing tomorrow, September 29th, from Guangzhou. We trust the goods will reach you safely and give you every satisfaction.

兹通知，我们已于今日将 500 件仿古陶器和 300 件瓷器装"飞云"轮，该轮将于明天（9 月 29 日）从广州出发。希望货物安全抵达并令您满意。

3）We are pleased to inform you that your order No. 443 has been shipped by S/S "CHANGHE", sailing on June 7 form Shanghai to New York.

我们很高兴地告诉你方，你们的 443 号订货已装"长河"轮，于 6 月 7 日从上海起航前往纽约。

4）Unless otherwise instructed，we will ship the goods by the first boat available toward the end of this month.

除非另有指示，我们将把货物交第一艘可订到舱位的船只于本月底运出。

5）The goods have been packed and marked exactly as directed，so that they may be rushed to the wharf for loading on the "TOKYO MARU".

货物已严格按照要求包装妥当，并刷好唛头，以便尽快运至码头，装上"东京"号商船。

6）The goods are to be shipped in three monthly lots of 20 tons each，with separate bills of lading for each lot.

货物分 3 个月装运，每批 20 吨，每批货物开具单独的提单。

2．To Mention the Enclosed Shipping Document

1）Enclosed please find copies of following documents：……

随函附上以下海运单证的副本：……

2）According to the terms of the contract，we forwarded you by air a full set of non-negotiable documents covering this consignment.

我们已按照合同条款的规定，将有关该批货物的一整套不可转让单据通过航空邮寄给你方。

Similar structures：

In compliance with the terms of the Sales Confirmation，
As stipulated in the contract，
Under the terms of the relative L/C，
In accordance with the stipulations of our agreement，
In the light of your specific conditions，
Since the contract is for November delivery，

we are sending

you under separate cover a full set of ...

3. To End the Letter With Goods Wishes.

1）We shall be pleased to hear in due course that the consignment has arrived safely and in good order.

希望早日听到货物安全抵达，完好无损的消息。

2）All items were individually examined before being packed and we trust they will reach you safely. We should be glad if you would unpack and examine them as soon as possible after delivery，and in the event of any breakage，notify us at once.

所有的货物在包装前都经过了逐一检查，我们相信它们能安全抵达贵处。收货后，请尽快开箱检查，如遇货损，请立即通知我方。

3）We are sure you will find the shipment satisfactory and we look forward to more opportunities of serving you.

我们相信这批货物能令您满意，并期待再次为您服务。

Writing Tips

Structure of an Advice of Shipment：

➤　Part 1：Inform the buyer the delivery of the goods and state the details of the shipment，such as

1）Contract No. /Order No. /LC No. ，

2）the name of the goods /Article No. ，

3）quantity of the order，

4）name of vessel，

5）ETD，ETA，

6）departure port/ arrival port

7）….

➤　Part 2：List the shipping documents enclosed within the advice.

➤　Part 3：Close the letter with good wishes that the goods will reach safely，or thank the buyer for patronage and look forward to repeat orders.

⑤ Field Exploring

➤ **Supplementing Useful Sentences**

ship，shipping，shipment

● Ship：*v.* 装运

1) to ship goods by S. S.（M. V.）由……轮装运货物

Please try your utmost to ship our goods by s. s. "Peace" which is due to arrive at Hamburg on 8 May，and confirm by return that the goods will be ready in time.

请尽力用"和平"号轮装运我方货物，该轮预定于5月8日抵达汉堡。请函复确认货物将按时备妥。

2）short ship：少装一些(货物)

Can we short ship 5 tons? 我们能少装5吨吗？

3）to be transshipped（at）转船

e. g. We have pleasure in notifying you that we have shipped today by m. v. "Milk Way" 200 cartons of children shoes. They are to be transshipped at Busan and are expected to reach your port early next month.

兹通知已由"银行"轮发运200箱儿童袜子。此货物将在釜山转船，预计于下月初到达你方港口。

● shipment：*n.* (1)装运　(2)装运的货物

date of shipment 装运日期

port of shipment 装运港

transshipment 转船

partial shipment 分批装运

advance shipment 提前发货

postpone shipment 推迟发货

e. g.

1）We are glad to inform you that the goods you ordered are ready for shipment. Please let us have your instructions for shipping marks and dispatch.

我们很高兴地通知你方所订购的货物已备妥待运，请告知唛头及装运要求。

2）We have inspected the shipment that arrived on the s. s. "Orient".

我们已检验了从"东方"货轮卸下的货物。

3）Owing to the delay in opening the relative L/C, shipment cannot be made in May as contracted and should be postponed until June.

由于相关信用证的开立延迟，无法按合同约定于 5 月发货，发货时间将延至 6 月。

4）If you desire earlier delivery, we can only make a partial shipment of 50 tons of rice in July and the balance of 50 tons in August.

如果你方要求提前装运，我们只能于 7 月装运其中的 50 吨大米，其余的 50 吨将于 8 月装运。

● Shipping 装运的 *adj.*

shipping company	船务公司
shipping port	装运港
shipping day/date	开船日期
shipping instruction	装运指示
shipping advice	装运通知
shipping mark	运输标志，唛头
shipping space	舱位，吨位
shipping document	装运单据

e. g.

1）We are sending you herewith a full set of copy shipping document.

现附上全套装运单据副本。

2）Please book the necessary shipping space in advance to ensure timely dispatch of the goods ordered.

请预订所需的舱位以保证及时装运所订购的货物。

● **Bill of Lading**

The ocean Bill of Lading (sometimes referred to as a BOL or B/L) is a document issued by a carrier to a shipper, acknowledging that specified goods have been received on board as cargo for conveyance to a named place for delivery to the consignee who is usually identified. It is one of the most important documents for handling over of the goods, claiming for compensation, and settling payment.

A through bill of lading involves the use of at least two different modes of transport from road, rail, air, and sea. It is an essential document in making a shipment. The standard short form bill of lading is evidence of the contract of carriage of goods and it serves a number of purposes:

• It is an evidence that a valid contract of carriage, or a chartering contract exists;

• It is a receipt signed by the carrier confirming whether goods matching the contract description have been received in good condition (a bill will be described as *clean* if the goods have been received on board in apparent good condition and stowed ready for transport);

• It is an evidence of ownership of goods described, and when made out "to order", it becomes in practice a negotiable instrument, used as security for loans and other purposes.

➢ **E-commerce Dialogue**

广州蓝尔迪塑料制品有限公司外贸员小林与美国客户 Smith 的在线聊天记录，回复客人关于运费的询问。

Smith（Buyer）：Hi，I'm interested in your product. How is the shipping fee calculated?

Lin（Seller）：Hi! Thanks for your interest. Shipping fees depend on the weight and destination. How many units would you like to purchase，and where is your shipping address?

Smith（Buyer）：I want to buy 5 units，and the address is in New York，USA.

Lin（Seller）：Got it. We offer express shipping，with a base fee of ＄20，and an additional ＄5 for each extra kilogram. For 5 units to New York，the shipping fee would be around ＄35.

Smith（Buyer）：I see. Would it be cheaper if I choose sea freight?

Lin（Seller）：Yes，sea freight is cheaper but slower. It's about ＄15 for base，plus ＄3 per kilogram. For 5 units，it would be around ＄25.

Smith（Buyer）：That's more economical. What if I buy 10 units，is there a discount?

Lin（Seller）：For bulk orders，we do offer a 10％ shipping discount. So，for 10 units via sea freight，the total would be around ＄40，discounted to about ＄36.

Smith（Buyer）：Sounds good. I'll consider it and get back to you later.

Lin（Seller）：No problem. Feel free to reach out anytime. Let me know if you have any other questions or need further assistance. Happy shopping!

➢ **Foreign Trade Elite Literacy**

新时代的"钢铁驼队"——中欧班列

中欧班列（"CHINA RAILWAY Express"，"CR Express"）是由中国铁路总公司组织，按照固定车次、线路、班期和全程运行时刻开行，运行于中国与欧洲以及"一带一路"共建国家间的集装箱等铁路国际联运列车，是深化国家与沿线国家经贸合作的重要载体和推进"一带一路"建设的重要抓手。

中欧班列往来于中国与欧洲及"一带一路"沿线各国的集装箱国际铁路联运班列。铺划了西、中、东3条通道中欧班列运行线：西部通道由国家中西部经阿拉山口（霍尔果斯）出境，中部通道由国家华北地区经二连浩特出境，东部通道由中国东北地区经满洲里（绥芬河）出境。

随着经济的不断发展和国与国之间交流的加深，货物运输在两国的经济交往中显得尤为重要。在国际供应链持续紧张的条件下，中欧班列维持可靠平稳运行，解了许多企业的"燃眉之急"。特别是中国幅员辽阔，从海上或港口到西部地区的距离会比较长，而铁路运输具有节省时间、成本低的优势，很多欧洲客户都被吸引了。自2011年中欧班列开始运营以来，中国许多城市都开通了中欧班列，数量和频率都在稳步增加。

9万列！中欧班列"跑"出开行新纪录

古有丝绸之路驼铃声声，今有中欧班列车轮滚滚。

25日8时40分，伴随着汽笛声在西安国际港站响起，X8157次中欧班列缓缓启动，一路向西驶向波兰马拉舍维奇。

至此，中欧班列"跑"出开行新纪录：累计开行9万列！发送货物超870万标箱，货值超3 800亿美元。

这一纪录，是中欧班列成长为亚欧陆路运输新干道的有力见证，也是中国与世界经贸往来愈发紧密的生动缩影。

更硬核——

2016年至2023年，中欧班列年开行数量由1702列增加到超1. 7万列，年运输货值由80亿美元提升至567亿美元；开行万列所需时间由开行之初的90个月缩短为现在的7个月……

在国内，经阿拉山口、霍尔果斯、二连浩特、满洲里、绥芬河、同江北六大口岸出境的西、中、东三条运输主通道运输能力大幅提升，时速120千米图定运行线已达87条，联通中国境内122个城市。

在境外，巩固和稳定既有入欧主要通道的基础上，跨里海、黑海的南通道成功开辟，目前已通达欧洲25个国家223个城市，以及11个亚洲国家超过100个城市，服务网络基本覆盖欧亚全境。

更有料——

打开第 9 万列的货箱：镍钴锰酸锂、汽车配件、百货、液晶显示板等货物装得满满当当。

从开行初期的笔记本电脑、打印机等 IT 产品，中欧班列的运输货物品类目前已逐步扩大到服装鞋帽、汽车及配件、日用百货、食品、木材、家具、化工品、机械设备等 5 万余种。

"带货"种类日益丰富，更多定制化班列不断推出，邮政物资、木材、茶叶、食用油、新能源汽车等特色专列提供着高品质的国际物流服务。2023 年以来，电动汽车、锂电池、光伏产品"新三样"成为中欧班列运量新的增长点。

运得多还得跑得好，中欧班列的运行品质也在迈上新台阶。

当前，时速 120 千米的中欧班列最大编组辆数和牵引质量分别提高到 55 辆、3000 吨，单列平均运量较开行之初提升 34％以上，中国与欧洲间铁路运输时间较开行之初普遍压缩 5 天以上。依靠铁路快速通关业务模式，中欧班列全程通关效率和便利化水平明显提升。

更给力——

看看沿线国家的变化：中欧班列让更多电子产品、家电、新能源汽车等"中国制造"以更快速度、更优价格到达欧洲的同时，许多新的物流、工业、商贸中心和产业园区随之涌现。

因为中欧班列的开行，德国杜伊斯堡港吸引了上百家物流企业落户，创造了 2 万多个就业机会；波兰马拉舍维奇口岸站业务量成倍增长，极大促进了当地经济社会发展。

与此同时，义乌小商品通过中欧班列销往世界各地，黄山茶叶、永康五金等地方特色产品也走出国门……

中欧班列还带动了我国内陆城市对外开放，一些不靠海不沿边的城市依托中欧班列，逐步发展成为对外开放新高地。例如，重庆外向型产业产值实现年均 30％增长，郑州现代国际物流中心建设得到有力支撑。

中欧班列的开行为沿线国家的百姓带去实实在在的获得感，也为国内企业"角逐"海外市场打开了一条便捷通途。

未来，"钢铁驼队"越织越密和越铺越广的线路图，将扩展越来越大的"朋友圈"，创造更多新机遇。

7 Practice

❶ Complete the Following Sentences in English.

1) We are pleased _____ inform you that we have booked freight _____ m. s. "Milky Way" _____ ETD _____ the 25th July.

2) With reference to our order No. 263 for 1,500 electric fans, _____ _____（我们希望提醒你方装运期已临近）.

3) We assure you that we shall _____（发货）on the specified date in your order.

4) _____（但我们订货时），we pointed out that punctual shipment is of importance.

5) It is regrettable that shipment is _____（过期、延迟）for more than two months.

6) This consignment of artificial flowers will be packed in 10 wooden cases, _____（每箱尺寸为 5×6×8 英寸，重约 50 磅）.

7) We will ship the captioned goods by the first _____（可订到舱位的）boat toward the end of this month.

8) You will _____（及时接到通知）when shipment of your order is effected.

9) We trust that you will make necessary arrangements to ship the goods within the _____（在原先规定的时间内）.

10) The goods are being prepared for shipment and will be loaded on m. s. Changlong tomorrow, _____（截止收货）.

❷ **Translate the Following into English.**

1）离港时间

2）到达时间

3）装运港

4）到达港

5）尺寸

6）你方应尽一切努力在信用证规定的时间内装运。

7）合同规定本月底之前发货，但如果你方能提早发货，我们将不胜感激。

8）766 号合同项下的化肥将装"飞云"轮，计划于本月底起航。请为此批货物购买保险。

9）兹通知 1234 号订单名下之货已于 11 月 30 日装直达船"红星"号，有关货样已于该轮启航前航空寄给你方。

10）关于你方第 80 号订单项下的 500 台缝纫机，我们已于 11 月 30 日装"东风"轮运出。相信该批货不久即可抵达你处。

❸ **Translate the Following Sentences into Chinese.**

1）Please send us by return full instructions for the 200 cases for Cairo，as to contents，values，consignee and who pays all the charges.

_____

_____

2）Enclosed you will find the bill of lading and invoice of the cotton fabrics ordered，amounting to ＄5，520，to be shipped by s. s. "Milk Way" with ETA at the end of this month.

_____

_____

3）We have shipped the goods per m. v. "Twilight" as instructed by yourself，and enclose herewith an invoice and B/L，which we hope you will find in order.

_____

_____

4) According to the terms of Contract No. 318，shipment is to be effected by the 20th Jan. , and we must have the B/L by the 31st at the least. We trust you will ship the order within the stipulated time as any delay would cause us no little inconvenience and financial loss.

_____

_____

❹ **Translate the Following Letters into Chinese.**

Letter 1:

Dear Mr. Rott，

Re: Your Order No. 3884

We acknowledge with thanks the receipt of your L/C No. G-103. Now we are pleased to advise you that the 20 metric tons of soybeans under the captioned order have been shipped on board s. s. Haiying which is scheduled to sail from Guangzhou on March 20 and due in New York on about April 30.

To facilitate your taking delivery of the goods，we are enclosing copies of the following shipping documents，each in duplicate:

Invoice No. GW-235

Packing List No. GW-264

Certificate of Origin No. 539

Non-negotiable Bill of Lading No. EKH-103

Insurance Policy No. 2948

Survey Report No. FR 293

新
编
外
贸
函
电

We hope this shipment will reach you in perfect condition and look forward to your further orders.

Yours sincerely,

Letter 2:

Dear Sirs,

We are very anxious to know about the shipment of our order for 5,000 pieces surfboards.

According to the terms of Contract No. SA568, the shipment is to be effected by June 23, 2022. However, up to now we have not received from you any information concerning this lot. We recall that when we placed this order we've stated explicitly the importance of punctual execution of this order. As the selling season is rapidly approaching, we shall appreciate it very much if you will arrange shipment as soon as possible, thus enabling the goods to catch the brisk demand at the start of the season.

Please do make serious efforts to get the goods dispatched with the least possible delay. Otherwise, we shall be compelled to cancel this order.

Yours faithfully,

❺ **Writing Practice.**

Situation 1 Draft a letter on behalf of Guangzhou Import & Export Corp. to Max & Co. in USA, urging shipment with the information given below:

(1)广州进出口公司从美国麦克斯公司进口了 50 台 HFH-311 型机器，订单号为 556；

(2)按照合约，所定货物应在 7 月和 8 月两批次等量装运。现一个月已过去，买方未收到任何消息；

(3)买方在订货时已经指出按期交货极为重要，因为其已经答应客户保证在 7 月底交第一批货；

(4)希望卖方在 8 月底之前把两批货一起运来，否则将可能取消订单。

Situation 2 Suppose you are the manager of Sunflower Export LTD. Write an Advice of Shipment in English to your customer with the information given below：

　　来信收悉，在收到你公司信件之后，我们立即与制造厂取得联系，催促他们赶快交货。因为他们迟迟不复，装船期不能肯定，我们在上个月没有答复你方的信件，深为抱歉。

　　经过再三努力，上述货物已装船完毕，信息如下：

- ·　商品名称：熊猫牌照相机，型号 HNT56
- ·数量：2 000 台
- ·总金额：1 789 800 美元
- ·船名/航次：Seagull /SW-256
- ·提单号：PBA056
- ·预计出发时间：2024.11.3
- ·预计达到时间：2024.11.20
- ·出发港：深圳盐田港
- ·随附相关单据副本：发票 XW2161，提单 MK211，装箱单 JFC7048，原产地证明 No.7-245

新编外贸函电

Module 8 Complaints, Claims and Adjustments

1 **Learning Objectives**

微课：解决投诉的正确态度

Upon completion of this chapter, you should be able to:

- determine whether a letter is a complaint or a claim;

- write different types of adjustment letters accordingly and appropriately;

- grasp the phrases and sentence patterns used frequently when writing an adjustment letter;

- know the skills to say "No." politely;

- communicate effectively with clients regarding after-sales problems online.

2 **Warm-up Questions**

- Question 1: What are the differences between a complaint and a claim?

- Question 2: How to reply politely to various complaints and claims?

3　Background Knowledge

微课：不同种类的理赔信

Complaints and claims will be made when one party of a deal is not satisfied with the other after receipt of the delivery. Goods shipped may be inferior in quality or damaged; shipment may be delayed; and sometimes wrong goods are sent. Under these situations, the companies suffering losses will write to complain or claim.

Replies to complaints or claims should be made promptly after receipt of any of that kind. No matter how trivial the complaint is, taking it seriously should be the basic attitude of the receiver. Of course, looking into the matter mentioned by the complainer is necessary before accepting compensation requests. After investigation, you should write an adjustment letter to the customer expressing apologies and raise your compensation plan, if your company caused the losses. If it is not a fault on your part, you have to write a polite letter to deny the customer's requests. In such a case, think twice before your writing in order not to make the receiver misunderstand you are shifting blames on others.

1. Differences Between Complaints and Claims

Complaints and claims are different in fact. A complaint is a written or spoken statement in which someone says he or she is dissatisfied or unhappy about something, while a claim is a demand for monetary compensation, a refund or replacement.

2. Two Types of Complaints Made by Importers

Genuine Complaints will be made under the following conditions.

(1) Wrong goods have been sent;

(2) The quality is not satisfactory;

(3) The goods delivered are damaged or late;

(4) Prices charged may be excessive, or not as agreed.

Market Complaints are complaints which are not in accordance with facts but from unfriendly intentions.

(1) The buyer finds fault with the goods intentionally as an excuse to escape from their contracted obligations;

(2) The buyer finds fault with the exporter and refuses to take delivery since they have found other suppliers with lower prices or the goods arrived are not popular at his market for the present.

3. The Claimed/Claimee and Claimant

The party who is responsible for a claim is the claimed/claimee, while the party who lodges the claim is the claimant. Losses or damages in foreign trade are not only confined to exporters and importers. Generally speaking, the claimed can be any one or two of the following parties.

(1) **Insurer**

The insurer is responsible for the following:

• Goods suffer losses or damages in transit because of the risks insured against;

• Other reasons stipulated in the insurance policy in which the insured can ask for compensation.

If the insurer is held responsible for the losses, the claim incurred is called "Insurance Claim".

(2) **Carrier**

The carrier is responsible for the following:

• Short-landed;

• Goods missing;

• Rough handling;

• Others.

If the carrier is responsible for the losses, the claim incurred is called "Transportation Claim".

（3）**Traders**

The seller is responsible for the following：

- Non-delivery or part-delivery；
- Delay in delivery/shipment；
- Inferior or wrong quality；
- Wrong quantity；
- Insufficient packing；
- Non-fulfillment of contract；
- Discrepancies in specification.

The buyer is responsible for the following：

- Refuse to open or delay in opening an L/C；
- Delay in payment；
- Commission unpaid；
- Failure in entering into contract；
- Non-fulfillment of contract.

If the trader is held responsible for the claim，the claim is called "Trade Claim".

4. Different Replies to Different Complaints or Claims

Adjustments differ in reply to complaints or claims according to different conditions. There are three possible cases：accepting the other party's claim completely；making adjustments to the other party's request；rejecting the other party's request completely.

Module-Related Correspondence

Letters Concerning Complaints，Claims and Adjustments.

- ➤ Letters concerning accepting a claim
- ➤ Letters concerning making adjustments to the other party's request
- ➤ Letters concerning rejecting a claim

新编外贸函电

微课：投诉与索赔信分析　索赔理赔信函结构与表达

⑤ Case study

Case 1

广州蓝尔迪塑料制品有限公司（Guangzhou Landy Plastic Products Co.，Ltd.）外贸业务员 Leo 收到了英国客户 Cathy 发来的关于泳池喷头（Swimming Pool Nozzle）发货延期的投诉函，并即刻回函答复，解决对方所提出的问题。

Letter 1：Complaint for Late Delivery

Hello Leo，

Hope you are doing great.

With all due respect，we have to complain about the late delivery of swimming pool nozzles.

The mentioned goods haven't been received until last week resulting in a delay of 2 weeks. The goods were supposed to arrive on March 14，and we had agreed on this before we reached this deal.

To our regret，similar occasions have happened two times in recent months. Our business cannot be carried on under such conditions，and we deem it necessary to make our feeling known. Without your punctual delivery，we won't be able to deliver the goods to our customers. Your late delivery has definitely harmed our further cooperation.

We hope you can understand our difficulties.

Thanks，

Cathy

Cathy

Common Expressions

- complain 投诉
- punctual 按时的

Useful Expressions

- with all due respect 恕我直言
- late delivery 发货延迟
- under such conditions 在此条件下
- harm our further cooperation 损害了进一步合作

Letter 2：Accepting a Claim for Late Delivery

Dear Cathy，

This is Leo from Hope Plastic Products Co. ，Ltd. in China. Thank you for telling us your dissatisfaction with late delivery.

It is our mistake to delay your order due to the peak season and labor shortage before the Spring Festival holiday. We apologize！

I know your urgent demand for promotion. After checking with our boss，we plan to deliver 30% of goods by air and the rest 70% by sea for the latest order. Therefore，you would receive 30% earlier than your schedule，and 70% roughly 1 or 2 weeks later.

Please reply ASAP. We have to check with forwarder urgently for arranging the delivery.

Best regards，

Leo

Leo

新编外贸函电

Common Expressions

- delay 延迟
- promotion 促销

Useful Expressions

- late delivery 发货延迟
- peak season（销售）旺季
- labor shortage 人工短缺
- check with forwarder 与货代确认
- arrange delivery 发货

Writing Tips

Structure of Letters to Accept a Claim：

➤ Firstly, confirm the receipt of the complaint or the claim，and apologize for any inconvenience or losses caused；

➤ Secondly，state the investigation process，and explain the adjustment plan；

➤ Lastly，express hope that they will accept your adjustment plan.

Case 2

广州伟力责任有限公司（Guangzhou Great Power Co.，Ltd.）外贸业务员 David 收到了澳大利亚客户 Peter 发来的投诉函，反应电池短量一事。David 立即调查了订单情况，致歉并说明短量原因，婉拒对方的索赔要求，提出新的赔偿方案。

Letter 1：Claim for Short Shipment

Dear David，

I am writing to inform you that the goods under order No. 2639/L have not been supplied correctly.

新编外贸函电

On 2 April 2024 we placed an order with your firm for 12,000 ultra super long-life batteries. The consignment arrived yesterday but contained only 1,200 batteries.

This error put our firm in a difficult position，as we had to make some emergency purchases to fulfill our commitments to all our customers. This caused us considerable inconvenience.

I am writing to ask you to make up the shortfall immediately and allow us 30% reduction on the invoice amount. Please ensure that such error will not happen again. Otherwise，we may have to look elsewhere for our supplies.

I look forward to hearing from you by return.

Yours sincerely，

Peter

Peter

Common Expressions

- consignment 货物
- shortfall 不足

Useful Expressions

- make some emergency purchases 进行紧急采购
- fulfill our commitments 履行承诺
- allow us 30% reduction on the invoice amount 在发票金额上减免 30%
- hear from you by return 收到回函

Letter 2: Making Adjustment to the Claim for Short Delivery

Dear Peter,

Please accept our apologies for the error made by our company in filling your order No. 2639/L.

You ordered 12,000 ultra super long-life batteries, but we sent only 1,200. This was due to a typing error.

The balance of 10,800 batteries was dispatched by express courier to your company this morning and will arrive in one week.

We regret to say it's too hard for us to accept your request for 30% reduction on the invoice value, because our profit margin is really small. Since we value your business, we would like to offer you a 10% discount off for your next order with us.

We look forward to receiving your further orders and assure you that they will be executed correctly.

Yours sincerely

David

David

Common Expressions

● dispatch 发货

● due to 由于，因为

● balance 结存，余款

● profit margin 利润率

新编外贸函电

Useful Expressions

- fill your order 执行订单

- by express courier 通过快递

- we value your business 重视您的业务

- offer you a 10％ discount off 给您 10％的折扣

- assure you that they will be executed correctly 向您保证它们将被妥善履行

➤ **Writing Tips**

Structure of Making Adjustments to the Other Party's Request：

- Firstly，confirm the receipt of the complaint or the claim，and apologize for any inconvenience or losses that have been caused；

- Secondly，explain why the adjustment to the request is made and why it is a reasonable settlement for both parties；

- Lastly，express the hope that they will accept your adjustment.

Case 3

广州格丽斯纺织品责任有限公司(Grace Textile Co.，Ltd.)外贸业务员 Alan 收到了英国客户 Cora 发来的关于毛毯包装不良的投诉函。她在信中提到部分外包装箱破损，内部的毛毯被弄脏，要求赔款或换货。Alan 对此事进行了调查后认为破损并非包装不当所致，礼貌拒绝了索赔要求。

Letter 1：Claim for Improper Packing

Dear Alan，

Our order No. KL-293 for 500 woolen blankets was received on October 15.

But we regret to say that 11 cartons were found broken and the blankets in them were soiled. This was obviously due to improper packing.

新编外贸函电

Needless to say，we have suffered a great loss from this as we cannot possibly deliver the merchandise in this condition to our customers. We，therefore，have to ask you to give us a 15％ allowance on the invoice value，or we will return the soiled blankets to you and ask for replacement.

We hope you will give our suggestion your most favorable consideration and let us have your decision at an early date.

Sincerely yours，

Cora

Cora

Common Expressions

● woolen blanket 毛毯

● soil 弄脏

Useful Expressions

● improper packing 包装不当

● give us a 15％ allowance on the invoice value 在发票的基础上给与 15％的折扣

● we will return the soiled blankets to you 我们把脏的毛毯退还给你方

● ask for replacement 要求换货

● We hope you will give our suggestion your most favorable consideration. 希望您能对我们的建议给予最积极的考虑。

Letter 2：Rejecting the Received Claim for Inferior Packing

Dear Cora，

We regret to learn from your letter of October 18 that 11 cartons of blankets shipped under your order No. KL-293 were found soiled and we are required to grant you a 15% allowance on the invoice value of the order.

We took your case seriously and have looked into the matter in detail. The packing department of our company informed us that the blankets were properly packed first in waterproof paper and then in double thickness of canvas as stipulated in the contract. Furthermore，the clean B/L covering the goods indicates that they were received for shipment in apparent good condition. Therefore，we are certain that the damage must have occurred through careless handling in transit.

Such being the case，we are afraid that we cannot accept your request. We would advise that you take up the case with the shipping company and have the claim settled to your satisfaction.

Sincerely yours，

Alan

Alan

Common Expressions

- grant 同意；准许
- waterproof 防水的
- canvas 帆布
- B/L 提单

Useful Expressions

- inferior packing 劣质包装
- looked into the matter in detail 彻底调查此事
- packing department 包装部
- in double thickness of canvas 双层帆布
- in apparent good condition 保存完好

231

- through careless handling 装卸不经心
- in transit 在运输途中

Writing Tips

Structure of Letters to Reject Complaints or Claims

➢ Firstly，express your thanks to the other party for telling you his or her dissatisfaction；

➢ Secondly，reject your responsibility for the problem leading to the complaint and state the reasons for the rejection；

➢ If a third party (another person or organization) is to blame，direct the complainer to that party；

➢ Lastly，write a concluding paragraph aiming at retaining the goodwill of the customer.

The skills to say "No." politely

➢ Begin with a reference to the date of the original letter of complaint；

➢ If you deny the request，don't state the refusal right away unless you can do so tactfully；

➢ Express your concern over the writer's troubles；

➢ If you deny the request，explain the reasons why the request cannot be met；

➢ If you deny the request，try to offer some friendly advice；

➢ Conclude the letter politely in hopes that you will continue doing business with them.

6 Field Exploring

➢ **Supplemental Expressions**

1. We have just received the 50 cases of chinaware shipped by s. s. "Yuanyang" under our order No. 617，but regret to inform you that cases

No. 15 and No. 20 were broken and their contents were badly damaged.

我们已收到贵方通过"远洋号"运来的第 617 号订单中 50 箱瓷器，但很遗憾地通知您 15 号和 20 号箱破损，里面的货物严重受损。

2. The green beans under the S/C No. 549 dispatched on August 10, 2023 have arrived at our port yesterday，but we regret to say that they were found to be below the standard stipulated in the S/C.

第 549 号销售合同下的绿豆于 2023 年 8 月 10 日运出，并于昨天抵达我港，但很遗憾地发现其质量低于合同中所规定的标准。

3. Referring to our order of September 16 for 50 metric tons of zinc sheets，we haven't received any news on the shipment from you since we placed the order one month ago.

关于我方一个月前，即 9 月 16 日订单下 50 公吨锌板，自从下单后就没有收到任何有关发货的通知。

4. I'm writing to complain about the inaccurate logo printing.

我写此邮件的目的是投诉贵公司将我们的商标印错了。

5. The quality of the goods shipped under our order No. 102 has been found not in conformity with the agreed specification.

我们发现我方第 102 号订单项下运抵的货物质量与不符合约定的规格。

Similar structures：

On comparing the goods received，we were surprised to find that they

are not the same as your sample.

do not correspond to the sample.

are below the standard we expected from the sample.

are not up to the sample we received from you.

are far from being satisfactory.

are the worst goods we have received from you.

6. Upon examination，we found that many of the goods were severely damaged，and the whole parcel is quite useless to us.

检验后，我们发现很多商品已严重损坏而且整批货物对我们毫无用处。

Similar structures：

We are sorry to say that	five bales were seriously damaged owing to negligent packing.
	you have sent us a substitute article instead of what we ordered.
	the content is not up to the percentage agreed.

7. We regret to point out that a shortage in weight of 200 pounds was noticed when the rice arrived.

我们遗憾地指出，大米到达时发现短重 200 磅。

Similar structures：

After inspection of the shipment，we found that

> it was 26 boxes short.
>
> 50 cases weight short by from 10 to 15 pounds.
>
> you have short－shipped this consignment by 40 kilos.
>
> there is a shortage of 270 kilos，though the packing remains intact.
>
> case No. 20 only contains 40 toy cars instead of 50 on the packing list.
>
> some items on your invoice have not been included.

8. A thorough examination indicated that the broken bags were caused by improper packing for which the suppliers are definitely responsible.

经彻底检查表明，破袋是由于包装不良造成的，为此供货商应负责。

Similar structures：

We regret to say that the goods were badly damaged

> apparently attributable to improper packing.
>
> owing to negligent packing.
>
> through faulty packing.
>
> because the bag is not thick enough.
>
> due to insecure packing.
>
> because the packing inside the carton was too loose (insufficient).

9. The quality of the goods is so poor and unsuitable for this market. As the whole parcel is quite useless to us，we ask you to refund us the invoiced value and the inspection fee as per the statement of claim enclosed.

货物质量低劣，不适合本地市场需要。由于整批货物对我们毫无用处，请你方退赔发票金额和检查费，详见所附索赔清单。

10. We have examined the goods duly received and found that the packing was soaked (saturated，wet through).

我们检查了按时到达的货物，发现包装已浸湿了(浸透)。

11. We are to say that the patterns are uneven in places and the coloring varies.

布匹花色不均匀，颜色也不一致。

12. The goods were packed loosely in the case without sufficient padding，thus causing the breakage of the articles.

箱内货物包装松散，缺少足够的填充物，导致货物破损。

13. There is a discrepancy between the packing list and your invoice.

装箱单与发票不一致。

14. 16 boxes were found split open.

16 个盒子裂开了。

15. The inferior quality of these soybeans has caused considerable difficulty to us and it is hard for us to dispose of them，even at a rather low price.

这批劣质大豆给我们带来极大的困难，即使以极低的价格也很难销售出去。

16. We had the sewing machines repacked before selling them to our end-users，which inevitably resulted in extra expenses amounting to US $350.

我们在将这些缝纫机卖给终端用户前不得不重新包装，因此导致我方额外支出 350 美元。

新编外贸函电

17. We should be glad to hear of the allowance you prepare to make to meet the case.

我们希望得知贵公司准备给予的赔偿，以便解决此事。

Similar structures：

Our customers say that they would oblige us by retaining these goods

---

if you will reduce the price，say，by 10%.

at a reduction of 5% on the invoice amount.

only at a substantially reduced price.

should you grant us 10% allowance.

if you can allow us a 5% compensation.

in case you can make us a reduction of 5% in the price.

---

18. In view of this，we have to return the faulty washing machines to you and ask you to replace them.

鉴于这种情况，我们不得不将有缺陷的洗衣机退回给贵公司，并请贵公司予以调换。

Similar structures：

Under these circumstances，we

have to return the goods to you at your expense.

shall have all the defective parts replaced at your expense.

request you to dispatch a duplicate shipment within one month.

are sending you a list of the inferior goods for your replacement.

shall hold the goods at your disposal pending your reply.

19. We have to lodge a claim against you for $ 500 due to the delay, because these goods are seasonal.

因为这批货物是季节性的，我们不得不因为货物延迟交付向你方索赔 500 美元。

Similar structures：

We are compelled，therefore，to

| place our claims hereby before you as follows. |
| have to claim on you for $ 2,000. |
| ask for a compensation of £ 54,000. |
| claim $ 780 for the value of the parcel against you. |
| request you to make up for the loss of $ 45,230 we sustained. |

20. This delay will surely cause us a loss of business，so we must receive these goods by the end of next month.

这种延误肯定会导致我们业务上的损失，因此我们必须在下个月底前收到这批货物。

21. Although the quality of these goods is not up to the usual standard of our industry，we will accept them if you can reduce the price by 3%.

尽管这批货物质量未达到我们行业的一般标准，但如果你方能降价 3%，我方愿意接受货物。

22. We hope you will eventually take into consideration our future business relations and let us have your remittance in due course.

希望你方最终能顾及我们未来的业务关系并及时汇付赔款。

Similar structures：

In order to resume our business cooperation，we deem it imperative for

you to	have this matter straightened out(解决) at once.
	pay attention to the adjustment of these errors.
	make a prompt settlement of this claim before our new orders.
	view this matter in the proper light and settle the claim immediately.
	effect a full settlement of our claim at your earliest convenience.

23. Please give our claim your favorable consideration.

请对我方的索赔予以积极的考虑。

24. We will appreciate it if you could look into the matter，and let us know your decision.

如您能调查此事，将不胜感激，并请告知您的处理方案。

25. Please look into this matter at once and take urgent measures to ensure nothing like this will happen in the second and third lots.

请尽快调查此事，并采取紧急措施保证第二、第三批货不会再出现此类问题。

26. We very much regret to learn from your letter of May 25 that you are not satisfied with the dress materials supplied under your order No. MP-115.

从贵方5月25日的来函中得知，您对第MP-115订单下衣料并不满意，对此我们深表歉意。

27. We have received your letter of 8 May together with the report showing that 20% of the lot were defective goods.

我们已收到贵方5月8日的来函及随附的报告书，报告显示这批货物中20%为次品。

28. We are sorry to learn from your letter dated June 12 that 60 cameras were damaged.

我们很遗憾地从贵方6月12日的来函中获悉有60台照相机受损。

29. We apologize for causing you a good deal of inconvenience.

很抱歉给您带来许多不便。

30．We are extremely sorry for the late delivery of your last order.

对于您上一笔订单发货延迟我们深感抱歉。

31．We frankly admit that delivery was delayed，but it was really beyond our control and we are taking up the matter with the forwarders and will let you know without loss of time.

我们坦承，交货确实延误了，但这真的超出我们控制的范围。我们正在与货代联系处理此事，并将尽快通知你方进展情况。

Similar structures：

We are extremely sorry for this delay，which you will realize was

due to circumstances beyond our control.

due to the breakdown of a machine in our factory.

owing to an unexpected demand.

caused by a strike in our factory.

caused by a fire that held up our production for a fortnight.

due to the late arrival of the raw materials.

32．Upon receipt of your agreement，we will T/T ￡900， the amount of the claim，into your account with the Bank of China.

一旦贵方同意，我们会将索赔金额 900 英镑电汇入你方的中国银行账户。

33．The short-shipped goods will be forwarded together with your next order.

短装的货物将与你方下一批订货一道发运。

34．In the spirit of goodwill and friendship we agree to accept all your claims.

本着友好的精神，我们同意接受你方的全部索赔。

35．We are willing to take the materials back，and if we cannot supply what you want，we will cancel your order.

我们会收回这批材料，如果无法提供你方所需，我们将取消订单。

36. We will give you a reasonable compensation，but not for the amount you claimed，since we cannot see the reason why the loss should be 50% more than the actual value of the goods. Please reconsider the matter.

我方将给予贵方合理的赔偿，但不是贵方索赔的数额，因为我们无法理解为何赔偿要超过货物实际价值的 50%。请再次考虑此事。

37. We are not responsible for the damage. We do not think it would be fair to have you bear the loss alone，so we suggest that the loss be divided between both of us，to which we hope you will agree.

我们不应为货物破损负责。但让你方独自承担损失有失公允，因此我们建议我们双方共同分担损失，希望你方能够同意。

38. As your complaint does not agree with the results of our test，we suggest that another thorough examination be conducted by you to show whether there is any ground for claim.

由于你们的投诉与我们检查的结果不符，我们建议你方再做一次全面彻底的检验，以确定是否有理由提出索赔。

39. The short-delivered goods you alleged might have occurred during transit，and that is a matter over which we cannot exercise control.

你方提出的货物短交问题，可能发生在运输途中，而这是我方无法控制的。

40. The evidence you have provided is inadequate，therefore，we cannot consider your claim as requested.

你方提供的证据不充分，因此我方不能考虑你方的索赔要求。

41. We are not responsible for the delay.

迟误的责任不在我方。

42. We sincerely apologize for the trouble caused to you and hope this matter will not affect our further cooperation.

我们对于给您带来的不便深感歉意，希望这件事不会妨碍我们未来的合作。

43. Please accept my apologies once again for the inconvenience.

给您带来不便，请再次接受我方的道歉。

44. We assure you that every possible action will be taken by us to prevent a repetition of the same in the future.

我们向您保证会尽一切可能防止将来此类事情再度发生。

45. We apologize once more for any inconvenience caused and would like to assure you that each shipment will be carefully examined before delivery.

给您带来不便，再次致歉，向您保证发货前会仔细检查每批货物。

> **E-commerce Dialogue**

广州蓝尔迪塑料制品有限公司外贸业务员 Jone 与澳大利亚客户 Taylor 在线沟通，解决 Taylor 对于产品质量不满意的投诉。

Buyer（Taylor）：

Hey，Jone. I need to talk to you about the plastic anti-slip grilles（防滑格栅）for swimming pools of the recent order. They're not in good shape.

Landy（Jone）：

Hi，Taylor. Sorry to hear about that. Can you tell me more about the issues you're facing with the products?

Buyer（Taylor）：

Yeah，the plastic grilles we received are discolored（褪色）and have cracks. It's not what we expected at all. We're pretty disappointed.

Landy（Jone）：

I'm sorry for the trouble. Can you give me the order number and send me some photos of the defective products so I can look into it?

Buyer（Taylor）：

Sure，the order number is XYZ123. I'll send you the photos asap.

Landy（Jone）：

Thanks for that. Once I have the photos，I'll get our quality control team on it. We'll work on fixing this ASAP and find a solution for you.

Buyer（Taylor）：

Thanks for taking care of this. We appreciate your help and hope to get this sorted out soon.

Landy（Jone）：

No problem. We'll do our best to make it right. I'll keep you updated on what we're doing to fix the problem. Thanks for bringing this to our attention.

Buyer（Taylor）：

We're counting on you to resolve this issue. We'll be waiting for your updates. Thanks for your help.

Landy（Jone）：

You're welcome. We'll keep you informed every step of the way. Thanks for your patience. We're committed to sorting this out for you. Let me know if you have any other concerns. Thanks for working with us on this.

➢ **Foreign Trade Elite Literacy**

如何有效处理客户投诉

处理客户投诉是外贸行业中不可避免的一部分，对于一位资深的出口公司业务员来说，如何有效处理客户投诉是至关重要的。这篇文章将分享一些关于应对投诉的策略和态度，希望对大家有所帮助。

第一，面对客户投诉时，我们要保持冷静和耐心。客户投诉往往是由于产品质量、服务不周或沟通问题等引起的，我们要以平和的心态去倾听客户的意见和抱怨，不要轻易发脾气或变得焦躁。只有保持冷静和耐心，才能更好地分析问题的原因，找到解决的途径。

第二，我们要及时回应客户投诉，不要拖延或置之不理。客户对于投诉往往希望得到迅速的回应和解决方案，因此我们不能让客户等待太久。在接到投诉后，立即与客户联系，表达诚恳的歉意，并积极寻找解决问题的方法。及时沟通和处理，将有助于减轻客户的不满情绪，并显示出我们的专业和责任。

第三，我们要始终以客户为中心，全心全意为客户着想。客户是我们的上帝，他们的投诉和意见是我们提升产品质量和服务水平的动力源泉。在处理投诉时，要善于倾听客户的需求和期望，以解决问题为己任，不断提升自己的服务能力，增强客户体验。

第四，我们还要建立健全的投诉反馈机制，及时总结分析投诉的原因和问题点，并加以改进完善。通过对投诉的深度剖析和总结，我们可以发现问题的根源，采取针对性措施，避免类似问题再次发生，提升工作的质量和效率。

第五，处理客户投诉需要具备良好的沟通技巧和解决问题的能力。在与客户沟通时，要用亲切而专业的语言表达，主动寻找解决问题的方案，并及时跟进和落实。在解决问题的过程中，要保持开放的心态，虚心接纳客户的批评和建议，不断反思自己的工作方式，不断提升自己的专业水平。

总的来说，处理客户投诉需要综合考虑客户需求、解决问题、改进服务等多方面因素，只有以积极的态度和专业的方法来应对，才能有效处理客户投诉，提升客户满意度，增强公司竞争力。

⑦ Practice

● **Complete the Following Sentences in English.**

1）It was found upon _____ that 10％of them are broken and some are badly scratched，obviously due to the _____ packing.

2)We are lodging a claim _____ the shipment _____ s. s. "White cloud" for short delivery.

3)We have to _____ about the poor quality of the cups we have just received.

4)In view of this, we have no choice _____ to _____ the faulty sets to you and ask for replacement.

5)A shortage weight of 100 kilos was noticed _____ arrival of the shipment.

6)The pens we received are not of the _____ model and size _____ we required.

7)It is obvious that apple juice was _____ weight before shipment. _____ such circumstances, we have to _____ a claim _____ you.

8)Fifty shirts were crushed or stained. _____ a result, they cannot be sold as new articles.

9)We _____ that the damage was not entirely your fault but feel that we should modify our packing requirements to _____ future losses.

10)We have to _____ on you _____ US＄50,000 as compensation.

11)The goods _____ Contract No. 123 left here in good _____.

12)We are very _____ to hear that goods you received are not _____ conformity with the quality of the samples.

13)Any complaint about the quality of the products should be _____ within 15 days after their arrival.

14)We regret that your claim _____ shortage cannot be _____.

15)Clients lodged a claim _____ you on the radios supplied by you _____ poor quality.

16)We will give your claim our favorable _____.

17)Please _____ _____ the matter as one of urgency and let us have your reply at an early date.

18）We regret _____ hear that several bags of the last shipment were broken _____ transit.

19）We will _____ the incorrect goods with right goods immediately.

20）As the articles were packed with the utmost care，we can only _____ that the damaged case has been stored or handled carelessly.

❷ **Please Translate the Following Sentences into English.**

1）经检查，我们发现商品的质量比样品差。

2）我们很遗憾地告知，我们收到的货物与你们提供的样品不符。

3）你发给我们的 30 箱计算机配件有问题。这显然是由于包装不当造成的。

4）你方提供的证据不充分，因此我方不能考虑你方的索赔要求。

5）短装的货物将与你方下一批订货一道发运。

6）错发的货物可以由下一班可订到舱位的轮船退回，但最好在你市场处理。

7）由于没有足够的证据，你方的索赔无法立足，我方认为进一步追究此事是毫无意义的。

8) 我们很抱歉给你们发去了次品，今天我们已经发去了替换的货物。

9) 经彻底检查表明，破袋是由于包装不良所致，供应商应负责任。

10) 对于不合格的衬衫，我们建议你们退回给我们，运费到付。

❸ **Please Translate the Following Letters into Chinese.**

Letter 1:

Dear Sirs，

We have just received the Survey Report from Shanghai Commodity Inspection Bureau evidencing that all drums of apple juice weight short by from 1 to 5 kilograms，totaling 300 kilograms. As the drums were intact，it is obvious that apple juice was short weight before shipment. Under such circumstances，we have to file a claim against you to the amount of RMB1,850 plus inspection fee.

We are enclosing the Survey Report and looking forward to your settlement at an early date.

Yours faithfully，

Letter 2：

Dear Sirs，

Thank you for your letter regarding your order No. 343，delivered last week.

We are sorry to hear of the breakage which occurred in transit. We pack our shipment with great care but there are occasions when the merchandise is mishandled along the way.

I have your inventory of the broken items. We shall make up a consignment of replacements which should reach you shortly.

Please hold the broken items for possible insurance inspection. I have lodged a claim with our insurer for the loss. We express our apologies for the inconvenience.

Yours faithfully，

④ Writing Practice.

Task 1. Please write to the supplier asking for compensation according to the following instructions.

　　1）确认已收到对方 3 月 5 日发来的 100 台机器；

　　2）告知对方其中三台部分受损；

　　3）请对方发来完好的机器更换这三台受损机器。

Task 2. Please write a reply for the letter you write in Task 1 by using the following information.

　　1）对货物受损表示抱歉；

　　2）提及机器受损可能是由于包装不当或是途中装卸粗心造成的；

　　3）表示你们将发去新的机器；

　　4）请对方把受损的机器寄回，运费到付。